THE AMERICAN
RIGHT WING

A Report to the Fund For the Republic

By RALPH E. ELLSWORTH and SARAH M. HARRIS

Public Affairs Press, Washington, D. C.

7139

INTRODUCTION

The late Dr. Harris and I undertook the preparation of this report because we felt that the American Right Wing was not being evaluated accurately.

We have not been either for or against this body of opinion. We have tried to establish the record so that others will have an adequate base from which to make their evaluations. We have endeavored, wherever possible, to let the Right Wing groups and individuals speak for themselves in their own words. We have been careful to make certain that their statements are fully representative of the individuals or groups.

The death of Dr. Harris in the summer of 1958 and my moving to a new position the same year has limited my ability to follow the literature and activities of the American Right Wing as closely as we had in the previous decade. And yet, as the conclusions of the report indicate, there have been no fundamentally new elements in the Right Wing movements, except the formation of the John Birch Society, in the past few years. The points of view, attitudes and modes of action have followed a basically consistent pattern since the end of World War II.

Although originally prepared as a report to the Fund For the Republic and initially issued in the Occasional Papers' series of the University of Illinois Library School, this work is not, of course, a report of either organization. The authors alone are responsible for the findings and interpretations presented in these pages.

The State University of Iowa Library maintains, for the use of scholars, the single largest collection of the writings of Right Wing organizations. Over the last fifteen years, these organizations were willing to give their publications to the library because they believed their ideas and statements were important. Anyone wishing to make a thorough study of the American Right Wing will want to consult the Iowa Collection.

RALPH E. ELLSWORTH

Director of Libraries
University of Colorado

When future historians come to write the history of the last few years, some may well be puzzled by the intransigence of the Republican years and the extreme caution of the Democrats. Some on the other hand, are likely to attach considerable significance to the fact that in the late fall of 1961 both Eisenhower and Kennedy found it necessary to warn the nation against the rising influence of the American Right Wing.

Many may wonder how it happened that during the Eisenhower years when press and airwaves rang with proposals for accommodating the emerging peoples of the world, when university studies offered unprecedented stores of knowledge upon which to base rapport, when church pronouncements united in a warm surge of brotherhood— how it happened that our elected representatives, our President and the Congress, stood firmly in the way of any forward movement, and spoke in 19th century terms of balancing the budget, restoring confidence, aiding the freedom-loving peoples, and dealing only with trustworthy nations.

Yet the fact was that the Congress, the Secretary of State, and to a lesser extent, the President, faithfully reflected an attitude that was stubbornly American, and one that reached from coast-to-coast in our country and from top-to-bottom in our society. It was a point of view that appeared only directly in the popular press and in the best-known journals of scholarship or opinion, and that was not thought to be important by the community of scholars, but it was a point of view that had a thousand voices of its own which spoke directly to the President and to each individual Congressman with remarkable persistence and energy.

They may wonder why, in the summer and fall of 1961, when the Berlin crisis was building up to a climax, President Kennedy found himself walking a very fine and unstable tight rope, with little chance to maneuver. Should he call the Russians' hand and force the reopening of East Berlin, he would run the risk of starting an all out nuclear war. Should he, on the other hand, come forward with compromises that in his, and his staff's, judgment might lead to long range settlement of the issues, he would run the risk of widespread and perhaps overwhelming criticism of being an appeaser and of lacking sufficient courage to stand up to Russia, as well as the risk of rebellion in the Congress.

1

It has been customary in recent years for historians and journalists to speak of the American Right Wing[1] as the lunatic fringe of the body politic; as a group of extremists small in number and absurd in pretensions; as isolationists, reactionaries, seditionists, native fascists, hatemongers, and, more recently, paranoiacs and schizophrenics, as though these deflating epithets will somehow insure that rightists shall have very little effect on the course of history. They are usually "exposed," and then dismissed as agitators and demagogues, products of psychological or sociological disturbance, unhappily necessary in a country given to free speech.[2] Even those who write about the rise of "the new conservatism" seem to feel that what they call right-wing "pseudo-conservatives" have had very little to do with this movement.[3] One frequently reads that since the censure of Senator Joseph McCarthy, rightist influence has dwindled to insignificance.[4] Yet an examination of right wing publications and activities, leads one to quite other conclusions.

Far from scotching the breed in its nest, the traditional name-calling campaign appears rather to have brought converts to the Right, and to have added a certain stature to those who have persisted in their work in the face of it. Some of the younger men still carry about with them copies of Ralph Lord Roy's *Apostles of Discord* and consider it an honor to acquire the autographs of any of those patriots who are pilloried in that book.[5]

There are approximately a thousand voluntary organizations in the United States today which may be called rightist, and which regularly publish or distribute great quantities of right-wing literature.[6] Some of these organizations are little more than a single dedicated individual, plus or minus a loyal wife, but others, such as the American Coalition of Patriotic Societies, claim as many as three million members.[7] While some groups are short-lived, others have worked vigorously for twenty years or more, and enthusiastic new organizations arise continually to replace those which have retired from the lists. The South today is a particularly fertile field for right wing sentiments, and it appears from the literature that the rightist organizer is enjoying better luck there than his left-wing counterpart.[8]

The publications which these groups sponsor range all the way from the earnest, smudgily mimeographed *Voice of the Hour* put out occasionally by Captain Edward Miles of Rally Point, U.S.A., to the handsome quarterly *Modern Age: A Conservative Review*, edited by Russell Kirk. There are many well-written and well-edited weekly, bi-weekly, and fortnightly journals of general political comment, such as William Buckley's *National Review*, Alice Widener's *U. S. A.*, Frank Hanighen's *Human Events*, Fulton Lewis, Jr.'s *Exclusive*, Merwin K. Hart's *Economic Council Letter*, Dan Smoot's *Report*, Edward Rumely's *Spotlight for the Nation*. There are monthly magazines as dignified as Leonard Reed's *The Freeman* and Robert Welch's *American Opinion*, as startling as Russell Maguire's *American Mercury*, as new as William Stephenson's *Virginian*, as old as Gerald L. K. Smith's *The Cross and the Flag*, as unilateral as William Dudley Pelley's *Valor* and *Over Here*.

Of the many newsletters reporting especially on Communist activities, some of the most vigilant are *Counterattack, Inform, The American Legion Firing Line, Freedom's Facts Against Communism*, the bulletin of the All-American Congress to Combat Communism, *Behind the Communist Line*, and the *Special Memorandum* from Universal research and Consultants. In addition there are the pamphlets and special reports put out by research organizations such as The Alliance, Capital Research Associates, and the National Republic—the last referred to by *Human Events* as Washington's most authoritative reference service—which also publishes a monthly survey. Less scholarly, but perhaps even more vigilant are the *American Nationalist, Closer Up, Common Sense, Don Bell Reports, The Revere, Grass Roots, The Greater Nebraskan, Task Force, Williams' Intelligence Summary*, and *Women's Voice*.

Many organizations such as the Minute Women of the U. S. A., the American Flag Association, the U. S. Day Committee, the National Renaissance Party, the American Education Association, We the People, the Organization to Repeal the Federal Income Tax, the Farmers' Liberty League, the American Public Relations Forum, Guardians of Our American Heritage, Campaign for the Forty-Eight States, For America, Pro America, and the Pasadena Anti-Communist League, publish regular bulletins and distribute pamphlets, flyers, and throwaways on special topics. Other groups organize for some temporary purpose—to deal with a local situation or put down a particular iniquity—but in so doing soon attract to their cause and reflect in their arguments the entire complex of right wing sympathies. Such groups include the Harvard Veritas Society, the Friends of the Aquinas Foundation at Princeton, the Alerted Americans of Plymouth Meeting the Boston Nutrition Society, Fighting Homefolks of Fighting Men, Citizens Against Fluoridation, the African Universal Church, the Indiana PTA Members Study Group, and the Massachusetts Women's Political Club.

There are also professional institutes which publish hundreds of serious studies on current legislation, such as the American Enterprise Association, the American Economic Foundation, and the American Good Government Society; on the theory and practice of conservatism, such as the Foundation for Economic Education and the new Princeton Panel; on specialties such as taxation, treated by Willis E. Stone's American Progress Foundation, and tariff, studied by the American Tariff League, which in 1958 issued a much discussed 117-page proposal to scrap the Reciprocal Trade Agreement.

There are the Americanism Commissions or National Defense Committees or Committees on Comunist Tactics of such groups as the Daughters of the American Revolution, the Sons of the American Revolution, the American Legion, and the American Bar Association, which frequently issue reports on political problems and distribute the writings of other rightists. There are the many timely booklets and brochures, all conservative in design, put out by the United States Chamber of Commerce, the National Association of Manufacturers, and the National Small Businessmen's Association; the house organs of innumerable businesses and industries such as U. S. Steel and Appalachian Coals; and the personal communications of such industrialists as Claude Efnor, who publishes the *Northwest Industrial News*.

There are radio commentators in great number who publish their broadcasts, such as John T. Flynn's America's Future, Clarence Manion's Forum, and Frank Kilpatrick's The American Way. There are newspaper columnists such as John K. Crippen and J. C. Phillips who write regularly and with conviction in the Des Plaines, Illinois, *Suburban Times* and the Borger, Texas, *News-Herald*. There are collectors who reprint and distribute editorials and news item of special significance such as Kent and Phoebe Courtney and Peck Associates. There are individuals who write frequent informative letters to Congress, and others—like Edith Essig, Lawrence Dennis, R. C. Rome, Gerald Barradas, Ralph Courtney, and F. J. Toohey—who send out mimeographed accounts of their considered opinions.

There are great numbers of blood-redemption Christians who populate all of the above categories and give them evangelical authority: Verne Kaub of the American Council of Christian Laymen, who has sometimes been called the Dean of the American Right Wing; Carl McIntyre of *Christian Beacon;* Harvey Springer of *Western Voice;* Billy Hargis of the *Christian Crusade;* Fred C. Schwarz of the Christian Anti-Communism Crusade; James Fifield of the Freedom Clubs and the televised *Lighted Window;* Bob Shuler of *The Methodist*

Challenge; Edgar C. Bundy of the Church League's *News and Views;*
C. O. Stadsklev of *Truth and Liberty;* John L. Rice of *Sword of the
Lord;* William D. Herrstrom of *Bible News Flashes;* W. C. and Sarah
Moore of *Herald of His Coming;* Max A. X. Clark of *National Chris-
tian Journal;* Howard E. Kershner of *Christian Economics;* Russell
and Ann Ackley of *Portions in Due Season;* F. Henry Sattler of *The
Malist;* Joseph Matt of *The Wanderer;* Stormy Jordan of the ironical
postcards.

A special offshoot from the conservative Christian branch comprises
organizations and publications devoted to the Anglo-Israel Message—
including the Anglo-Saxon Christian Congregation, the Anglo-Saxon
Federation (publishers of *Destiny*), the *Beacon Light Herald* of
William Kullgren, the British-Israel Association of Greater Vancouver,
the House of Prayer for all People, J. A. Lovell's *Kingdom Digest,* and
the National Message Ministry.

Recent additions to the collection are the multitudes of papers and
pamphlets published by rightist organizations in the South. Of
course there have always been conservative southern papers; two long
established ones with considerable individuality are Mary Cain's
Summit Sun and Ida Darden's *Southern Conservative* There are also
The Alarm, published by the Free Enterprise Association of West
Virginia; *The Small Business Review,* published by the American
Association of Small Business, Inc.; Horace Sherman Miller's *Aryan
Views;* Roy Harris's *Augusta Courier;* Parson Jack Johnston's *Georgia
Tribune;* Sherman Patterson's *Militant Truth;* George Benson's *Na-
tional Program Letter*; E. E. Williams' *Sons and Daughters of Free
Men;* and Thurman Sensing's Southern States Industrial Council
Bulletin.

In addition there is an extensive segregation and state's rights
literature published by various "Citizens Council." The *White
Sentinel,* a monthly newsletter put out by the National Citizens Protective Association of St. Louis, serves some of these Councils. Others
have their own papers, such as *The Councilor Newsletter* of the Association of Citizens Councils of Louisiana, Inc.; *The Citizens' Council* of
the Mississippi association; *The American Eagle* of Kentucky; *The
Crusader* of Florida; and *The Alabamian* of Alabama. There are over
550 local councils throughout the South, according to the *First National Directory,* and all of these distribute very interesting literature.
There is also the highly publicized Seaboard White Citizens Council
which, though denied recognition as rightist by *Right* and the *Virginian,* is highly praised by the National Renaissance Party and the

American Constitutional Party of Iowa; its organizer, John Kasper, has been defended by the Tennessee Federation for Constitutional Government and by Senator Russell of Georgia.[9]

Characteristic pamphlets distributed by the Citizens Councils include:

Tom P. Grady, *Black Monday.*

James F. Byrnes, *"The Supreme Court Must Be Curbed."*

John E. Carter, *Segregation.*

Eugene Cook, *The Ugly Truth about the NAACP.*

Earnest Sevier Cox, *Abraham Lincoln on the Question of Negro Colonization, The Races of Mankind, The School Situation at Clinton, Tennessee, Unending Hate.*

John W. Duggar, *God's Answer to Segregation.*

James O. Eastland, *"We've Reached Era of Judicial Tyranny"; Ford Foundation Finances Fund's Race-Mixing Drive.*

W. C. George, *Human Progress and the Race Problem.*

G. T. Gillespie, *A Christian View on Segregation.*

Billy James Hargis, *Integration by Force Is Not a Christian Crusade.*

Joseph P. Kamp, *Behind the Plot to Sovietize the South, The Lowdown on Little Rock.*

J. A. Lovell, *The Bible and Racial Purity.*

John B. Mason, *A Brochure on the 14th Amendment;*

M. M. McGowan, *Interposition or Nullification.*

Pat and Deane Mernagh, *Mammy Liza's Appeal to Her People on the Question of Integration in the Southern Schools.*

W. E. Michael, *A Tragedy of Errors; New Jazz Plot to Seduce Youth and Corrupt Races Exposed.*

Mathew Ravenshaw, *The Origin of the Black and White Races; Sickle-Cell Anemia.*

John Bell Williams, *Interposition, the Barrier Against Tyranny, Where Is the Reign of Terror?*

Accompanying the pamphlets are many handbills illustrated with photographs, cartoons, and drawings. These materials have wide circulation among rightist groups all over the country. Some have been read into the *Congressional Record,* reprinted in northern journals, and discussed in leading articles and editorials Andrew Lytle is probably right in saying that the South is not so much a place as "a state of mind within the Christian inheritance." [10]

Many have wondered if perhaps the segregation question may be the issue on which the Right will finally present a united front. Certainly it is dear to many hearts, and is sufficiently dynamic to hold together both rational and irrational elements—a necessity for any sort of nationalist mass movement which succeeds. In the recent past some division has occurred among rightists at the Constitution Day conventions of We the People and the Congress of Freedom, as well as in the Constitution Party which was organized in many states during the 1956 presidential election, and yet a considerable number of right wing groups have been interested in these bodies.[11]

Such a brief account hardly begins to describe the abundance and variety of right wing literature currently available, nor does it by any means do justice to the fertility and infinite proliferation of right wing doctrine, nor to the passionate partisanship of those who write about it. But it does make clear that the Right Wing has not withered away since the censure of McCarthy. It may be (and has been) argued by many that the groups described above are not homogeneous, and that to find common objectives in the publications of the American Bar Association and of Gerald L. K. Smith's Christian Nationalist Crusade shows a singular lack of discrimination. Many right wingers, in fact, have taken occasion to state their contempt for Smith's political opinions, though this has not caused them to reconsider any of their own identical views.[12] The Bar Association, furthermore, probably assumes, as does the American Enterprise Association, that it is neither right nor left, but entirely non-partisan and professional. The same may be said of the American Medical Association. Yet it appears that the publications of all these groups fall together in certain respects, and that these respects are right wing. No doubt it could be demonstrated that certain left wing tendencies also exist, but the preponderance of conservatism seems sufficiently clear to deserve more acknowledgement than it has received.[13]

No one has seen this more clearly than Bradford Martin and Willis Carto, editors of *Right* and the *First National Directory of Rightist Groups*. A monthly paper, *Right*, is a sort of exuberant gadfly which attempts to prick the Right Wing into full recognition of its far-flung power, and to unite all its followers in a surge toward the Capitol through a Liberty Lobby or Survival Commission. Right Wingers have by no means fallen into line; personality differences often loom larger than ideological agreement. Several years ago *Right* hopefully proposed a list of leaders who might command national enthusiasm: Bryton Barron, Admiral John G. Crommelin, General P. A. del Valle, General Bonner Fellers, John T. Flynn, Major George Racey Jordan,

Charles Lindbergh, General Douglas MacArthur, Dean Clarence Manion, General George Van Horn Mosely, John O'Donnell, Westbrook Pegler, Dan Smoot, General George E. Stratemeyer, Burton K. Wheeler, and General Robert E. Wood.[14]

Most of these people call themselves *conservatives,* and there seems to be no lexicographical reason to challenge their use of the term, or to water it down with *neo, pseudo, or ultra.* Historically, conservatives have always opposed change, and these conservatives oppose it no less. If they seem sometimes contrariwise to desire change instead, it is only temporarily, in order to remove that accretion of changes which have occurred in spite of them in the last twenty, fifty, or two hundred years, and which they have never accepted as legitimate. Some historians wish to reserve the term *conservative* for Edmund Burke, Alexander Hamilton, John Adams, and Winston Churchill, but they must surely realize that the style and grandeur of these archetypes can never be characteristic of the rank and file, and that their basic dogmas are amply present in the writings of current believers.[15] In some ways, *conservative* seems a more adequate designation than *rightist* or *right wing,* since the latter suggest to some minds a splinter group, and it appears that the literature described does not proceed from a splinter group, but represents a large portion of American opinion.[16]

At least one lifelong conservative would disagree flatly with this conclusion. Richard Whalen has declared that it would be impossible to collect or to examine the writings of conservatives, because, as he said, "Real conservatives do not write." There is a kind of half truth in this statement which ought never to be lost sight of. (It is even possible that real leftists do not write either.) For it must be remembered that many of those whose works we examine in these pages are, first and foremost, writers, and writers of extraordinary energy and devotion. Talent is unevenly distributed among them, and whereas some are lively and capable, others are little instructed. Those who are well-trained are often pedantic. Those who are exciting are often uninformed. Some write in a highly emotional vein, others with a kind of leashed invective. Some are barely literate. They all tend to be repetitive and, like other coteries, are faithful readers of each other's works.[17] A lack too many share is any real acquaintance with the great books of the world or the special disciplines of learning that have developed in the universities. Frequently they seem unable to distinguish between the able scholar and the doctrinaire educationist, shunning them all as eggheads and intellectuals. Indeed, it is the proud boast of one young conservative that "There are *no* conservative intellectuals." [18]

The truth appears to be that there are many conservative intellectuals, but that when they actually do write, they are usually called "radicals of the right" and separated at once in the public mind from the "real" conservatives who do not write—from Taft and Bricker and Knowland and Silent Calvin Coolidge. John Fishcher, in a recent article, "Why Is the Conservative Voice so Hoarse?" observes that "it is impossible to coax a manuscript out of any conservative of standing," and notes that former Secretary of the Treasury Humphrey, whose "intellectual radiance is blinding," "recoiled in horror" when asked to state his views in a book. Fischer finds this unfortunate but clearly if Humphrey did write a book, Fischer would see him as an extremist—one of that "small congregation of the faithful" whose emotional hunger, he feels, is fed by the *National Review*. One reason for this confusion is probably the fact that the ranks of the conservative intellectuals have been notably increased in recent years by an influx of reformed leftists who have brought with them their "editorial tone of humorless indignation, almost indistinguishable from that of the *Daily Worker*." Such writers as Ralph DeToledano, Ulius Amoss, Louis F. Budenz, and J. B. Matthews have swung full circle in their political beliefs but have maintained their polemical style. Others seem to have adopted such a style unconsciously, from perpetual scanning of Communist literature and of Russian news dispatches for "intelligence." [19]

However, such conservatives as Walter Lippmann, August Heckscher, Peter Viereck, Clinton Rossiter, and Richard Weaver are not accepted by most writers of the Right as their spokesmen. Neither have they ever identified their interests with those of the southern agrarians—Allen Tate, Caroline Gordon, John Crowe Ransom, Robert Penn Warren, or, until recently, Andrew Lytle—though some rapport has been established with Donald Davidson because of his aid to the Clinton Freedom Fighters. [20]

But there are others who are acceptable. Anthony Bouscaren lists some of them: Willmoore Kendall, Richard L. Walker, Gerhart Niemeyer, Robert Strausz-Hupe, Robert T. Oliver, Stefan Possony, Medford Evans, E. Merrill Root, William McGovern, Kenneth Colegrove, A. H. Hobbs, Sister Margaret Patricia McCarran, Ludwig von Mises, Godfrey P. Schmidt, Charles Tansill, William Stokes, Mark Graubard, Wladyslaw Kulski, Roman Smal-Stocki, Robert J. Kerner, Felix Wittmer, James Burnham, William Henry Chamberlin, Alexander St.

Ivanyi, F. A. Harper, Ruth Inglis, and George Huszar.[21] One might add John Beaty, David J. Dallin, Arthur Bliss Lane, John C. Caldwell, L. Brent Bozell, Garet Garrett, James Musatti, Thomas James Norton, Henry Hazlitt, Robert O. Jones, Orval Watts, Karl Wittfogel, and a great many others.[22]

Most of these men are professors, some are journalists, but all are writers, or as Eric Hoffer would call them, "fault-finding intellectuals." [23] They find much fault with what they call the Liberal Establishment, and it is true that liberals often deny them any standing in the world of ideas. "In the United States at this time liberalism is not only the dominant but even the sole intellectual tradition," Lionel Trilling says flatly in the introduction to *The Liberal Imagination* (1950). "For it is the plain fact that nowadays there are no conservative or reactionary ideas in general circulation . . . The conservative impulse and the reactionary impulse do not, with some isolated and some ecclesiastical exceptions, express themselves in ideas but only in action or in irritable mental gestures which seek to resemble ideas."

Trilling is generous enough to wish with John Stuart Mill that the wisdom of conservatives may increase, but many liberals are very pessimistic about this possibility, and in 1957 Martin Seymour Lipset, for example, found no improvement. Such attitudes are sufficiently familiar to right wingers, who appear at times to take a certain perverse gratification in their martyrdom. In her *Reading List for Americans,* Phyllis Schafly points out how many of the books and writers named were "blacklisted by publishers, reviewers, libraries and book stores," and how many of her "pro-American scholars" had to struggle against "boycotts and biased book reviews." It is for this reason that the Right has set up its own publishers and periodicals, according to conservatives, and now with the Freedom School, recently established in Colorado, it hopes to make some impression on the academic world also.[24]

II

Conservative writers characteristically unite in believing that they represent political individualism as opposed to the new collectivism. Traditionally this stand has often belonged to the opposition, and there are old-fashioned progressives today who make the same claim, calling for self-determination abroad, and for rescuing the small farmer and the small businessman from centralized industry at home.[25] Collectivists, furthermore, protest that they offer far more to the individual—to every individual—than do the individualists. Scorning to make common cause with either of these positions, however, the Right Wing establishes its own individualism in two ways. It opposes strong centralized government and it opposes all foreign entanglements.

It is not entirely clear why the American Right has so consistently fought against a strong federal government. Alexander Hamilton and John Adams defended it vigorously, so that although these men are much admired by modern rightists, they are quoted less often than Jefferson. Yet very few rightists believe, as Jefferson did, in the perfectibility of man. Most of them share a profound distrust of man's nature, and a general acceptance of the doctrine of original sin. As the British conservative F. A. Voigt explains it, ever since the French revolution (though one might as well say since the Renaissance), we have ignored God and put our trust in imperfect, sinful man. Utopians, do-gooders, one-worlders he says, simply will not face the fact of man's miserable nature, and so they are constantly undone by his inclination to break promises, spill blood, seize power, and enslave them. [26]

This is the tragic flaw in liberalism, agrees a reviewer in the *Times Literary Supplement,* that liberals "incline to the view that man is by nature set toward goodness, that he is almost indefinitely improvable, and that once the reasonable course has been pointed out to him his reason will embrace it. Liberals have never sympathized with the doctrine of original sin." [27]

One would suppose from these beliefs that liberals would feel the need for little government, and conservatives for much—that like Hobbes our rightists would hope to control man's natural wickedness by rigid laws and a powerful central authority that would direct all aspects of his behavior. Yet the opposite appears to be true. One wonders sometimes if this is only an appearance, and if the rightist really believes that men do need strong government, but that such government is most effective at the local level where he can keep a personal eye upon it; that he cannot trust any man with power as far away as Washington; and that the Congressman, by his removal from the immediate neighborhood, is already subject to alien influences and inevitable corruption.

"Government unlimited is at once the most diabolical, the most treacherous and the most uncontrollable force known to man," according to Robert B. Dresser. Understanding this fully, our Founding

Fathers, he says, established a limited constitutional government, reserving all powers not delegated to it "to state, respectively, or to the people."[28] "For some years past, however, the federal government has been encroaching steadily upon the rights and powers of the states,"—actually, "since 1933, when the philosophy of new dealism (latterly known as fair dealism and modern republicanism) first became a controlling force in Washington—when we embarked on the curiously crooked path that in twenty-four years, has taken us into a labyrinth of contradictory policies, into a morass of national debt, and into disastrous foreign policy failures." Or, as Verne P. Kaub writes: "Briefly, the American libertarian feels that the founders of our government set into operation a governmental form which should have been more closely adhered to than has been the case ... Those favoring and promoting the changes in governmental operation take the viewpoint that the 'industrial revolution' and other developments have made the original form of government out of date and unsuitable for use in this present era. The libertarian does not believe this. He is sure that governmental interference in the affairs of the citizens is not only unnecesary but unwise."[29]

To combat this strong federal government, the Right Wing opposes everything that contributes to it, beginning with the federal income tax ("the root of all evil," and straight out of the Communist Manifesto, according to Frank Chodorov, *Dawn,* and Orfit),[30] and proceeding through the resultant bureaucracy and statism that has led to federal regulation of labor, business, agriculture, interstate commerce, health, education and welfare, and even to government competition with private enterprise in as many as seven hundred different businesses as enumerated by Willis E. Stone of the American Progress Foundation. Stone has testified before Congress that the federal budget could be substantially reduced and taxes made negligible at the same time, if the government would close down these corporate enterprises.[31] Such proposed constitutional amendments as the Bridges-Byrd-Curtis Amendment to limit Congressional spending, and the Dirksen-Gwinn Amendment to limit the taxing power were heartily endorsed by the Right Wing, as was the Sadlak-Herlong bill to revise the tax structure.[32]

It is believed that to further temper inflation and depression, the budget must be balanced, the "sound" dollar restored, perhaps by raising the price of gold per pound, as suggested by Edward Rumely, or even by returning to the gold standard as proposed by George Racey Jordan (if it is possible to do so with the present ambiguous situation at Ft. Knox where foreign countries have more gold deposited than we do), but certainly by giving up the Keynesian idea of "full employment," which is basically inflationary and incompatible with free enterprise. An American Enterprise Association pamphlet describes fully "the waste, the sluggishness, loss of incentives, and the rigidity of the labor market that results from 'full employment' " [33]

Another inflationary spectre which haunts the Right Wing, probably first reported by Racey Jordan, is the irreversible incident of the moneyplates lent by our government to the Soviet government during the war, whereby United States money printed by the Russians is in permanent circulation, and "unscrupulous international Misplaced Persons" are using to "virtually steal" "theatres, hotels, and main street properties from real Americans." [34] No solution for this predicament has received any widespread acceptance.

Equally unsound, according to Rightists, is the social security system. Doomed to failure from the beginning, this system, it is pointed out, now pays out more in benefits than it takes in taxes, robs the worker of the right to spend his money as he wishes, and plagues the employer with endless paper work. According to Dr. Lewis Aleson at the 1957 Philadelphia meeting of the American Medical Association, social security is "part of a mad and unreasoning rush into the cold and leprous arms of the welfare-police-slave state." The American Medical Association has consistently fought against social security, and in fact against all federal and state proposals to improve the national health by legislation. [35]

Nor does the Right Wing ostensibly take any comfort in government contracts and subsidies to business as a substitute for low taxes and high tariffs. It is opposed to handouts and giveaways, and for this reason hates the Big Deal of the modern Republicans as much as any of those other deals that preceded it. It would not, of course, consider the tidelands oil a giveaway, but simply a case of the federal government's actually keeping its hands off private property. [36]

Neither does it in general share the modern Republican's complacence in the face of centralized labor unions. The popular statement, "We're all New Dealers now," is vigorously challenged by Frederick Nelson, Associate Editor and editorial writer for the *Saturday Evening Post.* [37] Encouraged by the Congressional investigation into the Teamsters' Union and hoping against hope that the public might become aroused at the political machinations of the United Automobile Workers, conservatives have worked hard for Right-to-work laws in every state. Senator William Knowland fought for such a bill in Congress, and campaigned on this issue for the governorship of California. The free rider has every right to do his own bargaining, it is held, and has no real reason to think he may be less successful than the organized union bargainers, who are, of course, unmitigatedly collective.[38]

There is still much concern on the Right about the character of the blue-collar worker, and most hold with Herbert Hoover that it can only deteriorate under the welfarism of Big Government and Big Labor. The American Economic Foundation's editorial, *The Welfare State and Honesty* says that "when there is neither morality nor reward to stimulate an honest day's work, the full fruits of the economy will never be realized." Those who feel with Edmund Burke that the poor need only "patience, labor, sobriety, frugality, and religion," are not impressed with either the People's Capitalism or the Social Gospel, and speak often of bread and circuses.[39] It is here, perhaps, that they feel most bitterly the defection of the National Council of Churches, which they claim is impressively pro-labor. Time was when organized religion could be counted on to support free enterprise and to recognize its rewards as the outward and visible signs of inward and spiritual grace.[40] Perhaps rightists should accept the change as a natural manifestation of Big Religion.

But at least among the fundamentalists there are still allies. The fundamentalists have never accepted economic security as a reform measure, and often view it as an actual deterrent to personal salvation. They consequently oppose all reform of societies from the outside, and believe with F. A. Voigt "that every attempt to establish the Kingdom of Heaven on Earth establishes a hell on earth." [41] With Congressman August Johansen they deplore "salvation by apropriation," and some even go so far as to feel that the "Biggest Hindrance to Gospel Is Not the Iron Curtain But the Plush Curtain." Or as Edgar Bundy puts it, "Jesus Christ was not interested in lobbying before Pilate, Agrippa, or Caesar's government for betterment of social, economic, or political conditions ... He left his followers no legacy in the form of material comforts and a high standard of living. He left them only a cross and an eventual crown, to be obtained through persecution and martyrdom."[42]

George Thomas goes even further in *The Greater Nebraskan*: "If Jesus returned today, it's doubtful if He could look for any help from our modern churchmen ... He would be blacklisted for creating confusion and enmity among the races. They would be shocked by His references to Heaven, Hell, Blood and Sin." [43]

One can only agree that these people speak much truth. But why, then, one may properly ask, do they spend so much time writing political tracts? William Herrstrom has an answer for this, too, in *Bible News Flashes*: "People who think they believe in prayer... think it is wrong to pray for the 'welfare' of any city or the future of their country or their children... that is 'politics' and they tell us, Christians should have nothing to do with politics... Let all Christians keep silent... while Satan takes over the whole world with no protest from the Christians... So they voted for a stooge of the Communist Party who occupied the White House for some years and set the stage for the destruction of America... a danger which is now imminent. This could have been prevented if the 'cowardly' preachers had not become the 'Devil's Doormats' " " Yet it appears from other issues of *Bible News Flashes* that only rightist preachers should speak up. The uncowardly social gospel preachers who do speak up run further risk of becoming doormats.

Perhaps even more widespread in the Right Wing has been vigorous opposition to federal aid to health and education, since every man in the street feels that he understands these problems, even though he may be puzzled by economic and religious issues. Few indeed are the rightist groups which have not fought against the Public Health Service and its promotion of mental health, and of fluoridation of city water to retard tooth decay. Each of these issues has in fact become so crucial and so elaborately spun out, that it is difficult to tell now whether or not the initial opposition sprang, as might be supposed, from an aversion to socialized medicine. Certainly this point is not stressed in the literature. Looming far larger than any serious consideration of national health or even of government interference is the legend of a Soviet plot, or perhaps two plots, to conquer America. Of fluoride, we are told that the Russians depended upon it during World War II to keep their prisoners docile, and that its use in city drinking water will cause a slow poisoning which will gradually reduce us to robots. The great concern among conservatives over this poisoning, which they declare results in stiff backs, paralyzed legs, arthritis, intestinal disorders, stunted growth, kidney stones, loss of fertility, and slow death, is in startling contrast to their absolute conviction that the effects of nuclear fallout are negligible. It is also pointed out that many Russians, and people known to be associated with Communist organizations, have positions in the Public Health Service, and on the state Boards of Public Health."

Many of those who are most concerned with the effects of fluoride were also exceedingly distressed over the advent of the Salk polio vaccine, and have been vociferous enemies of the American Cancer Society for a long time, and vigorous promoters of the Hoxsey method of cancer treatment. Others have protested with J. Richard Feeley the use of food additives, hormones and the like, and have seen in all these measures the hidden hand of the enemy. There are also several groups of right wingers who promote health foods and health cosmetics, and such devices as Wilhelm Reich's "orgone energy accumulator." [46]

A characteristic statement on the fluoride plot and related tangents, distributed by the Gold Star Sons and Daughters of the American Revolution, appeared originally in *Free Men Speak*:

"George Indest, Jr., nationally known authority on fluoridation of water supplies, warned that the March of Dimes Salk polio vaccine will be administered to nine million school children by the same Association of State and Territorial Health Officers that is knowingly conspiring with the U. S. Public Health Service in the fluoridation-cancer plot.

"He pointed out that there are so many Russian-born doctors and dentists in our Public Health Service and in state health offices that it has been commented on in the Congressional Record; and that the U.S.P.S. and Surgeon General belong to the World Health Organization, 'a sort of medical United Nations to which Russia also belongs.' He stated that 'in some countries the public might become a little alarmed to find Russian doctors pouring rat poison in the public water supplies.'

"Parents were warned to keep their children away from the Salk polio shots ... Most parents don't realize that the school children of today represent our Army and Navy ten years from now. If millions of them can be innoculated, let's say with a radioactive substance that will cause cancer in a few years, why ten years from now the communists could walk in and take over our nation of old men." [47]

The diabolical nature of this conspiracy is suggested by William Herrstrom: "A far-sighted saint in her eighties, who had spiritual discernment far beyond that of most present-day Christians, wrote me stating that the powers of darkness were attemping to dope the drinking water in her city with the poisionous 'fluorine' which destroys the body and mind and especially the will-power to resist that which is wrong. She was old and feeble—unable to carry the fight to the front. She inquired where she could find a prayer group who could pray for the deliverance of her city." [48]

But John Monk, after quoting a typical remark from one M. Conan of Phoenix, Arizona ("Of course the slow poisoning of our people by fluorine would make the Communists happy. Then Russians could take us over without a struggle and we would not know what it was all about") declares firmly: "The Communists have nothing to do with it and neither does Russia. It is a very small item in Zionism's Protocols Plan of world conquest, both Russia and the U.S. are to be victims." [49]

The mental health program is also interpreted as a conspiracy, and often as one aimed directly at the Right Wing. This interpretation is found in articles by George Todt which were read into the *Congressional Record* by Senator Barry Goldwater. The Alaskan Mental Hospital Law which was passed in 1956 distressed many conservatives because it appeared to them to create a kind of Siberia to which political prisoners might be sent against their will, and it seemed clear to them that these prisoners would be right wingers. There had already been the classic cases of Lucille Miller, the Finn twins, A. R. Fitzpatrick, Anthony Marino, Kathryn Deats, and, of course, most famous of all, Ezra Pound—all right wingers whose political views unquestionably figured in determining their assignment to mental hospitals. Lucille Miller, in her paper *The Green Mountain Rifleman,* first called the Right's attention to the incarceration in 1945 of Ezra Pound as a political prisoner at St. Elizabeth's Hospital in Washington, D.C. [50]

John Kasper, a forthright Right Winger who has been much in the press, testified before a Senate Committee in 1956 that Pound was not insane, as certified, but was being punished for treason, for which he had never been tried in any court. Psychiatry, Kasper added, was a Jewish invention, and thoroughly un-American. Both Pound and Kasper himself have been defended by the American Civil Liberties Committee, on the ground that their civil liberties have been invaded, and it appears that in Pound's case the indignation of the Right, if sometimes a little histrionic, is certainly entirely reasonable. [51]

Characteristic of such reaction is the comment of an American Legion writer who quotes the following passage from an American Friends' Service Committee *Bulletin* (May, 1952) : "What makes a super-patriot a super-patriot? The following paragraphs speculate on the forces within, which drives such men and women. It is an expression of a belief that understanding may enable us to help them. The super-patriots are clearly afraid. Being adults, they must rationalize their fears. They may call it "concern for country."

They see a threat to the nation in the U.N. and the UNESCO (or whatever) because these groups include strangers—people of different culture, language, religion and race. But their fears, to cause such hysteria, must be related to something far more basic than "flag" or "country". This is the *purest paranoid delusion*: "I have hundreds of lurking, secret enemies!"

Explaining away the fancied enemies one by one will never relieve the condition for the person who is deluded. A friendly and loving attitude toward each mentally ill person is basic to being helpful. He feels the enemies and invents and seizes upon the person or group to be the enemy, to explain the feeling to himself: "The A. F. S. C. implies that 'super-patriots' who refuse to be conditioned (to world understanding) are mentally ill. Presumably such mentally ill people should have the benefit of medical treatment as prescribed by world-minded individuals who are not afflicted with the 'disease' of patriotism."[52]

Compare the above question to Harry A. Overstreet's statement in *The Great Enterprise* (1952): "A man, for example, may be angrily against race equality, public housing, the TVA, financial and technical aid to backward countries, organized labor, and the preaching of social rather than salvational religion ... Such people may appear normal in the sense that they're able to hold a job and otherwise maintain their status as members of society; but they are, we now realize, well along the road toward mental illness."

This statement by Dr. Overstreet is quoted by Edith K. Roosevelt in her article, "Bats in the UN Belfry?" "What Dr. Overstreet describes, of course," she says, "is the prototype of millions of conservative people everywhere." Even more disturbing is her report that Povl Bang-Jensen, who served as Deputy Secretary to the UN Special Committee on the Problem of Hungary, and who refused to deliver to the United Nations a list of Hungarian witnesses against Communism, was suspended as an officer of the UN and is now spoken of as not "rational," but as "aberrant," "odd," hence inevitably unreliable and incapable of telling the truth and exercising good judgment.[53] Or as Mrs. Alice Widener puts it, Povl Bang-Jensen stands officially accused, by an UN Committee, of conduct that departed markedly from normal and rational standards of behavior." [54]

One learns, too, that Walter Reuther has stated that Senator Barry Goldwater needs a psychiatrist. This, of course, is exactly what Senator Goldwater would expect him to say. It appears that the

Alaska Mental Hospital may eventually need its entire land grant after all.[55]

Conservative opposition to federal aid to education has been absolute, and here again a whole tangle of issues unite in the shadow of conspiracy. There is first of all the basic opposition to strengthening the federal octopus or authorizing additional expenditures. We have no need of federal scholarships, conservatives declare, since thousands of available scholarship dollars go unclaimed every year. Neither do we need buildings, since the children are already too much spoiled with gymnasiums and swimming pools. Floyd D. Golden, Vice Chairman of the American Legion's Americanism Commission in 1956, reported to Congress the Legion's opposition to Federal Aid for Education. He spoke of the danger of undermining state and local responsibility; of powerful centralized authority leading to thought control and to infiltration by the communist conspiracy; of higher taxes.[56]

Led by the Legion's attack in New York on the social science texts of Harold Rugg, and in Pasadena on UNESCO materials in the schools, almost every one of the thousand right wing organizations described here has been fighting progressive education, the National Education Association and John Dewey ever since the war's end. It is felt that any federal support of education is bound to be support of progressive or Big Education, and that federal aid must therefore be fought on these grounds also. The recent discovery by the American press that Russians receive a classical European education has not altered the contention of right wingers that "Progressive Education is Reducation," nor the assumption that the godless, treasonable, obscene and illiterate curriculum which they find in present-day American schools has enabled the communists to control Russia and will serve them equally well here.

Milo F. McDonald, President of the American Education Association, explains the historical relation between communism and progressive education as many conservatives see it, in a pamphlet called *"Progressive" Poison in Public Education* (1951). He characterizes John Dewey's experiments at Chicago and his later teaching at Columbia Teachers' College as dangerous because of their emphasis on relativism and socialism—their "exaltation of the pupil and . . . Subordination of the teacher"—in what came to be called the "activity program." Dewey's activity program, McDonald tells us, was adopted by Lenin in 1917 as the official Russian school system, and remained in effect until Stalin's reorganization in 1932.

Lenin's aim, according to McDonald, "was the establishment of a totalitarian government. He saw in the activity program a means of realizing a new social order in Russia. He saw in it a weapon which he could use to make plausible to the large population of Russia . . . that rigid controls must be inaugurated if anarchy were to be prevented. He saw in the activity program a means of breaking down among youth respect for authority. He saw in it a means of destroying true scholarship. He saw in the theory of 'freedom of expression' a challenging of the authority of the teacher at school and of the parent in the home. He saw in the appeal to youth to settle their own problems, even those of love, of marriage and of sex relationionships, an opportunity of playing havoc with the deep religious convictions of the Russian people, indeed, with all the traditions of family and social life of Old Mother Russia and creating a new social atmosphere in which totalitarianism and despotic control would have a better opportunity to breathe and to grow to the full stature which he, in time, would come to enjoy . . . In his judgment of the consequences of the activity program Lenin proved himself to be a shrewd and correct planner."

By 1932 "it became evident that self-expressionism had produced undisciplined children and youth. It had produced lawlessness and anarchy . . . Stalin had achieved by means of Deweyism in Russia a situation which Lenin had envisaged. Now the use of police methods to curb the depravity among Russian youth would be approved by all residents in the Soviet whether they were Communists or not. Now was the time to institute such curbs and to ditch the activity program. Now was the time to emphasize the need for study in the schools; now was the time to reject the theory of self-expressionism without restraint and to substitute for it an emphasis upon discipline in the schools of the Soviet."

At this very time that Russia was introducing rigid controls into her school system, McDonald points out, the United States was adopting Dewey's activity program here, under the encouraging eyes of George S. Counts, a Dewey disciple who was in full accord with the purpose which the program had served in Russia and would serve here, —i. e., building of a new social order. Since 1935 the system has flourished, and education has suffered accordingly. "Are the children and youth . . . to become the tools of the Soviet in its effort to control the world?" McDonald asks. "Does totalitariansim threaten us and are our public schools a possible source of danger? Do we believe we are invincible and immune from sabotage? The planners are with us. They have with them 'progressive' poison. Our local schools are being destroyed by it. Let us hope all our citizens will awake and arouse themselves before it is too late." As J. Edgar Hoover put it in his much-quoted article in the *American Magazine,* "The Communists are after Our Minds." [57]

Other right wingers, however, see less danger from the overt communist conspiracy than from the "dupes, dopes and punks who are advocating abandonment of the Constitution of our Republic in favor of a mythical mess of repulsive Statism." Or as Dan Smoot says: "The real subversive movement in American schools has been led by people of good repute who, while not openly advocating communism or even socialism, have used our schools as a means of building a socialist America. Much of this has been fobbed off on parents and taxpayers under the labels of 'progressive' or 'modern' education." [58]

Conservatives holding these views have been quick to identify themselves with those teachers and educators who have recently begun to attack progressive education on other grounds. Arthur Bestor, Mortimer Smith and their Council for Basic Education, for example, have been cordially welcomed into the right wing movement by *National Review and U.S.A.* Although the CBE Bulletin has had nothing to say about Russian plots or the planned society, most of its comments are completely congenial to the conservative mind. The fact that CBE, seeking to strengthen the intellectual dedication of the schools, has attracted rightwing admirers who often describe themselves as anti-intellectual, is less paradoxical than at first appears, since both groups are identically opposed to the schools' concern with life-adjustment, permissive discipline, integrated problem approaches, and such dogmas in determining the curriculum as readiness and interest. Both groups distrust educational psychologists and indeed the whole hierarchy of educationists, and believe that additional financing, federal, state, or other, would do nothing for the schools but perpetuate a bad situation.

In addition to the questions of leftist indoctrination and illiteracy in ordinary schools, conservatives are much concerned with the further complication of racial integration in segregated schools. They are systematically opposed to it. Even northern conservatives have stood firmly against integration, again on the ground of federal interference with states' rights, and it is somewhat disconcerting to see how readily they speak of giving up public education altogether and rescuing the young from the tyranny of equality and fraternity for the sake of, as they say, individual liberty. They find the whole "civil rights" law a mere political maneuver to take away their "natural rights" to make free choices, and can see no possible motive for its adoption other than the meanest type of political self-seeking. Two right-wing heroes, William Knowland and Richard Nixon, have lost considerable prestige by their ambivalent support of this measure.[59]

Many interests enter into right wing attitudes here and become intricately interwoven. There is the old Know-Nothing bias against intellectualism mentioned earlier, which has always been restive under the national commitment to universal educational opportunity. There is the puritan notion that juvenile delinquency might be abated and a supply of cheap labor provided if many teen-agers were allowed to leave school and go to work. "Education, after all, was meant for those capable of being educated, not for those who at most can be led astray by it." There is the basically snobbish assumption that superior (and possibly one's own) children would be better off in private than in public schools, and that with the abolition of the latter, the state might arrange tuition for the former. There is the earnest desire of many, including teachers and educators of various convictions, to improve the quality of the educational offering, and to make more learning available for those who can handle it.[60]

Closely tied in with the conservative's disapproval of present-day public education is his dissatisfaction with the United States Supreme Court as presently constituted, or, as he usually calls it, the Warren Court. The Warren Court has generally become recognized by the Right as the most dangerous single aspect of the strong federal government which it so heartily opposes. It is seen as the enforcing arm of Big Government, and a bill introduced by Senator Jenner before his retirement proposed to curb its powers and distribute many of them to the separate state courts. This bill satisfied the Federation for Constitutional Government, *National Review, Human Events, Exclusive* and John K. Crippen's Ani-Communist League of America (though strangely enough, not the *Chicago Tribune,* which is against any limitation of powers); but other papers held out for impeachment of the justices, particularly the *Augusta Courier, Free Men Speak, Dan Smoot Report,* and the Pasadena Anti-Communist League's *Newsletter.* Many groups distributed copies of "A Resolution Requesting Impeachment of Six Members of the United States Supreme Court," by the General Assembly of Georgia, 1957. As Crippen put in his and Miller's statement before the Senate Internal Security Sub-Committee on behalf of the Jenner bill: "The 'Warren Court' has had damaging effects upon the FBI, the duly-constituted investigating bodies, upon the sovereignty of the states, and it has violated lawful precedent to an alarming degree." [61]

It is characteristic that the Director of the Anti-Communist League of America wishes to champion the FBI. It may seem surprising that groups which are so concerned about personal liberty, so fearful of the police state and of strong central power, so fully aware of the prevalence of conspiracy, have never feared the FBI or thought of it as other than their own fortress of strength and protection. This is probably because J. Edgar Hoover has so thoroughly identified his own political position with that of the Right, but it also speaks well for his organization and for the government it serves. [62] Even those on the Left, who have less cause to admire the director, have rarely accused the FBI of the kind of persecution with which they have sometimes charged Congressional committees.

But the Supreme Court is something else again. Clearly, according to the Right, it has fallen into the hands of the collectivists. As Senator James O. Eastland declares, "The greatest single threat to our Constitution is the presently constituted Supreme Court of the United States. In fact, the Court, by its decisions, has aided the cause of Communism." He then reviews the decisions of the Court, beginning with the unanimous Desegregation Decision of May 17, 1954, and proceeding through the many decisions relating to subversive activities, treason and sedition up to the present date, stating that "There are now pending before my judiciary committee more than 100 bills designed to cure or alleviate the effect of one decision or another that has been rendered by the Supreme Court." The Jenner Bill to Limit the Court's Appellate Jurisdiction in Certain Cases, as amended by Senator John M. Butler, was probably the best known of these. According to Fulton Lewis, Jr., Senator Jenner felt that "the Court is badly in need of an unequivocal Congressional chastisement as a preventative against future derelictions." [63]

Between Black Monday and Red Monday (days on which critical decisions were issued) there is little to choose, and much is said of this government of men rather than of laws. Especially resented is Chief Justice Warren's reference to Gunnar Myrdal's *An American Dilemma* as a basis for the integration decision. Eastland states that Myrdal and his sixteen assistants "have a long record of affiliations with Anti-American causes and the Communist conspiracy," and that "it is a final indication of the extent to which the Court has been 'brainwashed' by minority, even alien, pressure groups." [64]

"By that decision the Supreme Court handed to the central government a power it had never before possessed—the power to put its grasping and omnipotent hand into a purely local function ... It will not be long before the socialist revolutionaries will have what they want—control by the central government of what to teach and what not to teach." [65]

Many Northern writers sympathize fully with the South's desire to preserve segregation: Frank Chodorov in *Human Events* (March 30, 1957); James Ingebretsen in *Faith and Freedom* (March and April, 1956); Bradford Martin in *Right* (May, 1956); the South Deering, Illinois, *Bulletin;* Lucille Miller in *Southern Digest* (March-April, 1956). The Minute Women of the USA, Inc., distributed a speech by John Bell Williams; Marilyn Allen published two segregation pamphlets in her *I Love America* series; the *Revere* (September, 1956) gave an approving account of the revival of the Klan, and offered copies of Dixon's *Clansman and Leopard's Spots* for sale; the American Constitutional Party of Iowa distributed copies of John Kasper's ballad; Robert H. W. Welch wrote "A Letter to the South on Segregation" in *One Man's Opinion* (September, 1956); Leon DeAryan's *Broom* reprinted Mathew Ravenshaw's *Origin of the Black and White Races* (January and March, 1958); Aldrich Blake wrote the pamphlets, *The Civil Rights Revolution, Freedom of Choice, It Can Be Done; Closer Up* (January 10, 1958) made a special study of Sickle-Cell Anemia with photographs. Envelopes from both north and south are stamped "Remember Little Rock," and "Brotherhood by Bayonet." [66]

Of course, even more is said in the North, about the Court's "at least 15 decisions designed to put the meddling fingers of the federal politicans further into state affairs, and to completely break down all our defenses against the communist conspirators in our midst." John T. Flynn has made a simple proposal for handling this situation as well as a number of other awkward developments. "It is that all decisions of the Supreme Court, from 1937 to the date of the adoption of the proposal, should be declared to have no force and effect as precedents in judicial or other proceedings." This will "enable all future Supreme Courts, no matter how otherwise reformed, to disregard the usurpations of the Court in the last 20 years." [67]

The American Bar Association's Committee on Communist Tactics, Strategy and Objectives, reporting at a London conference in August, 1957, seemed almost as distraught as Flynn. It found that the Court was following the Communist Party line in at least fifteen important decisions: "If the courts lean too far backward in the maintenance of theoretical individual rights, the report stated, it may be that we have tied the hands of our country and rendered it incapable of carrying out the first law of humanity—the right of self-preservation." This report was quoted with relief by many on the Right, whereas it took an individualist from the Left, Gerald W. Johnson, to point out "The government is not human and does not possess the rights of humanity . . . the government has no interest other than protecting the right of the citizen to life, liberty and the pursuit of happiness." [68] Although this report was not circulated by the Bar Association, summaries of it appeared in many places, such as *The Cross and the Flag.* Subsequently the Bar Association published in its *Journal* an article by Frank B. Ober, "Communism and the Supreme Court," which makes essentially the same pronouncements in a somewhat more restrained manner, though not omitting to speak of the Trojan horse, the pseudo liberals who are the ready tools of the Communist conspiracy, and the fact that the FBI files should be kept inviolate. [69]

III

Since conservative Americans are so unalterably opposed to a strong federal government, one may be certain that they are even more suspicious of all forms of international collectivism. It is clearly one of the marvels of our time that the Congress passed the United Nation Participation Act; much credit for this must, of course, go to a conservative, Senator Arthur Vandenberg. For in the concept of a world forum the rightist is confronted not only with a dangerous form of centralization, but also with that other traditional aversion of individualism—foreign entanglements. It is a curious anomaly that the United States, which is planted from one end of the other with foreigners, should from the very beginning of its history have harbored such a primitive distrust of them. [70] Or perhaps it is for this very reason—that each generation has had to adjust to a new wave of immigration, bringing aliens into the very heart of every community— that hostility has never had a chance to ripen into either indifference or acceptance. The Puerto Ricans today have acquired the animosity formerly directed toward (but not yet entirely withdrawn from) the Germans, the Irish, the Swedes, the Italians, and the Jews. [71]

Many a right winger is frankly and firmly opposed to first-class citizenship for Negroes and hyphenated Americans—a term by which he often designates his first and second-generation countrymen. One of the primary virtues of the Smith Act for him is probably that it directs the denaturalization and deportation of subversives. The rightist is a staunch defender of deportation, and has taken a lively interest in the possibilities of repatriation, as it is called, of the American Negro. He defends with devotion the Walter-McCarran Immigration and Nationality Act, and sees any attempt to amend it as a contemptible bid for political power.[72]

Representative Francis E. Walter defends the national origins quota system on which the law operates, and its base year of 1920, chosen for establishing the total number of admissable quota immigrants. He finds particularly ludicrous the accusation that the law promotes second-class citizenship and racism, and declares that it removes both types of discrimination from the traditional American policy. If this is true, then Walter must certainly observe that two-thirds of those rightists who support the law are at variance with him on this issue. As Crete Anderson declared for the American Legion: "Our cultural background stems principally from Northern and Western Europe, and ... our institutions are rooted in Anglo-Saxon traditions." It is important to preserve these, and "to protect our country from penetration by those who would subvert it." Similarly the American Coalition of Patriotic Societies resolves against amending the immigration act, which is "a principal object of attack by Communists, hyphenated-Americans, one-worlders, intellectual pinks and politicians seeking to favor so-called nationality blocs." [73]

Parallel attitudes are seen in the publications of the American Defense Society and the Daughters of the American Revolution. The DAR's National Defense Committee distributes copies of an address by Richard Arens which states that 180 Communist-controlled organizations in this country are dedicated exclusively to the purpose of destroying the immigration act. The act must consequently be preserved. Any change is a victory for the enemy. The DAR's have, of course, been on record for some time "that no immigration over and above that provided under the present quota system shall be permitted into the United States." The *Small Business Review* urges the President: "Do not put anybody in an official position unless his parents were naturalized United States Citizens before he was born, and not less than second generation if possible." The America Action Council recommends that we pass a law that an "American-born Christian only can hold any public office," and has as its motto: "George Washington calls from everlasting light, 'See to it that ye put only Native Sons on guard this night' " [74] The Realpolitical Institute calls for "Immediate discharge of all alien non-Whites, members of the disloyal

Jewish Consensus, Internationalists, Pacifists, Communists, and Liberals from all local, State and Federal governments and Armed Forces."

Actually it must be apparent that those conservatives who call themselves libertarians and who desire individual liberty for every American simply do not consider Negroes and recently naturalized citizens Americans at all. Otherwise they could not possibly see in an extension of liberty to these people so peculiar an invasion of their own natural rights. Nor do they recognize the basically American contributions to national life which have been made by many of those with no known north European ancestor.[75]

Of course many of these contributions have been made in areas which the rightist already regards as suspect—areas which have been riddled with internationalism from the beginning, such as art and learning. All original (and consequently 'modern') work in painting and music, creative writing and scholarship, has always seemed alien and un-American to most conservatives, and frequently subversive and obscene.[76] There is a kind of justice in the claim, since it is true that art and letters of any consequence must always have a certain element of outrageousness—a certain unconservative quality—and a certain lack of regard for national boundaries and ideologies. That these qualities must also be present in science and scientists, whom Rightists had formerly considered their partners in the advance of industrial capitalism, is a discovery that brings them much discomfort today. Now scientists, along with artists, intellectuals, teachers, churchmen, labor leaders, bankers, diplomats, the universities and the foundations, must be watched with that eternal vigilance which is the price of liberty. It is a rather staggering burden.[77]

With this general attitude toward foreigners, even when naturalized, it is only reasonable for the Right Wing to deplore the establishment of United Nations headquarters in this country, for this has brought scores of untrustworthy aliens to our shores, and they have all got diplomatic immunity. Not only that, but it is believed that we have surrendered much of our national sovereignty to this irresponsible organization, and will surrender more as the months pass. "Take the United Nations out of the United States, and the United States out of the United Nations!" is the war cry of the Congress of Freedom, and of many other patriotic groups which look with despair at the mess we have got ourselves into. One cannot help sharing their wonder that so many conservatives voted for it. They find its "hideous glass House tha' Hiss built" a suitable encasement for the whole

heathen enterprise, and see as symbolic the fact that this building is
heedlessly planted on the spot where Nathan Hale declared his regret
at having but one life to give for his country. As Albert J. Lindsey
says, the United Nations is "in one sense a Red Trojan Horse. It
gives Godless world Communism a forum . . . we will not deny that
there are humanitarian aims in the Economic Council of this institution," he goes on to state, "but the basic principle is contrary to the
divine program of God. It is Satanic in its origin and if pursued, can
only bring us down the road eventually to our sorrow and destruction." [78]

Almost worse than our participation in the United Nations, however,
is our commitment, because of our opposition to the Soviet Union,
to foreign aid, to foreign military bases, to stationing troops abroad
(at the mercy of the Status of Forces Treaty), to Point Four programs
of technical assistance, to cooperation with foreigners in NATO,
UNESCO, GATT, ILO, to endless negotiations with the Soviet Union,
and to every other type of cooperative iniquity. For one who fought
the establishment of the St. Lawrence Seaway because it would "make
our Lake Michigan an International Body of Water," this situation is
almost more than can be borne. "Bomb Russia!" cries the irascible
Colonel Bluford H. J. Balter, and there are others who agree with
him. "Why," he asks, "did the Heavenly Father . . . give us the atomic
bomb? . . . to use it judiciously to destroy Communism . . . Bomb
Stalingrad and Moscow . . . The good Russian people will then be free."
Or as the American Council of Christian Churches puts it in a letter
to Congress: "There is a solemn responsibility resting upon the free
world to preserve and protect itself, and if necessary to use atomic
weapons first . . . it is better and just that people committed to an
anti-God system of the darkest tyranny be the victims of their own
folly." As Senator Styles Bridges says, "It is time we stopped per-
mitting Russia to assume that we will never act until she strikes
the first blow." [79]

Those on the right who are more cautious propose variously that
we either repeal the UN Participation Act, or that we expel the Soviet
Union and other communist countries from the UN, boycott trade with
these countries, and cancel U.S. recognition, meanwhile offering every
encouragement to such of these peoples as wish to revolt from communism. They propose further that we pass the Bricker Amendment limiting the President's treaty-making power, void the Status
of Forces Treaty, and renounce UNESCO, GATT, ILO, and Point
Four. In NATO we must take a more dominant stand, and refuse to

share nuclear secrets, economic support, or anything else with our parasitic allies. We should raise tariffs for the good of our industries, and give up all foreign aid except that which is essential for military purposes. (That there is little foreign aid of any other type still goes largely unrecognized.) Obviously the Right Wing is still dedicated to the old American First Approach which used to be called isolationist and which is now called unilateral. It wishes to crush communism by withdrawing from it the "mantle of respectability" which we have so far provided, and by silencing its voice in our forum. Naturally nothing appears more evil than the Russian proposal for a summit meeting. The first summit meeting was "deadlocked," J. B. Matthews tells us, referring to Christ's encounter on the mountain-top with Satan, and this "was an historic victory for the Kingdom of Righteousness, *because it was deadlocked."* [80]

"Foreign Aid Is Not Christian," either, we learn from Elgin Groseclose's article of that name. It is based on the Marxist assumption that economic conditioning will improve people and societies, whereas Christians know that nothing but personal redemption can ever improve them. "Our junketeering aid distributors, accepting the premises of Marxism, have created a reservoir of hate. Or as Spruille Braden says in the *Congressional Record,* "It is my conviction that the mutual-security program strikes at, and if continued much longer, may destroy our religion, our way of life, the Constitution, and, therefore, all decent and moral civilization ... Our foreign aid is counter to religion because, far too often, it is being employed for the benefit of Communists and fellow travelers whose aim is to destroy all belief in God over vast areas of the earth. This results from your and my hard earned dollars being given to the anti-Christ—to Communists like Tito or Gomulka ... What could be more utterly humiliating and shameful than ... to try to bribe these wretches to be allies and friends? ... Truly, foreign aid is a treacherous if not a treasonous, adventure." [81]

We have seen how the conservative's aversion to Marxism runs like a continuous thread through every expression of his political individualism, and it has consequently appeared to some writers that militant anti-communism is the distinctive doctrine of the Right Wing, and the great cause that binds disparate groups into an impressive contemporary movement. Certainly anti-communism was McCarthy's cause, and McCarthy, once the leader, is now the honored martyr, of the American Right Wing. Yet we must remember that anti-communism in America is by no means confined to the Right, and that those who fight it from the Left—including Paul Douglas, Sidney Hook, James Wechsler, Arthur Schlesinger, Jr., Max Eastman, Norman Thomas, and James T. Farrell, for example—though equally militant, do not demonstrate the same syndrome of interests and beliefs that we have sketched here as characteristic of conservatives. It would seem, on reflection, that the Right Wing's adoption of anti-communism as its *cause celebre,* though dating back to the very birth of Bolshevism in the 1919 pronouncements of the American Legion, and even earlier for those who fought with the Populists or against the Socialists and the IWW, was by and large an outgrowth of its historic distrust of foreign entanglements and of collectivism, and that consequently a cause could hardly have arisen which would have proved more completely suitable for it to embrace.[82]

This is the more clearly demonstrated when we remember that there is a long tradition on the Right of belief in the existence of an inter-national conspiracy of unscrupulous men or nations, possibly centuries old, which is destined to destroy our civilization. Archibald Roosevelt director of The Alliance, has called attention to the harm this notion has done to the Right, but the myth has continued to flourish in the more sensational papers, and often creeps unexpectedly into the least emotional of them. Variously identified as the Illumininati, the Mafia, the Jewish Cabal, the International Bankers, the Invisible Government, the Brotherhood, the Society of Freemasons, the Synagogue of Satan, and more recently as the B'nai B'rith or "Jewish Gestapo," the legends of this secret world government provide an ideal background for belief in a rigidly conceived communist conspiracy.[83]

We are all familiar, of course, with the real nature of communism. Communists and ex-Communists have reported a wealth of detail about it, and this has received an extraordinary amount of publicity in all American mass media. What is less advertised, though hardly through any fault of the Right Wing, is the manner in which inter-national communism conforms to the grand design of the ancient conspiracy. No one has stated this any better than Admiral John G. Crommelin, who announced his unsuccessful candidacy for the Gov-ernor of the State of Alabama with the following resolution:

"Whereas, None but the blind can fail to see and none but the dreamer will choose to deny that the present course of government is leading this State and this Nation to demoralization, mongrelization and bankruptcy, and

"Whereas, the key to survival is a thorough understanding of the Communist-Jewish Conspiracy, and

"Whereas, The satanic plot to mix the blood of the White Christian People of the South with negroes is directed and financed by the Communist-Jewish Conspiracy, and

"Whereas, Our great State of Alabama has been selected by the Communist-Jewish Conspirators as the proving ground for testing ways and means to carry out their plot, and

"Whereas, The ultimate objectives of the Communist-Jewish Conspirators is to use their world-wide control of money to destroy Christianity and set up a World Government in the framework of the United Nations, and erase all national boundaries and eliminate all racial distinction except the so-called Jewish race, which will then become the masters—with their headquarters in the State of Israel and in the UN in New York, and from these two communication centers rule a slave-like world population of copper-colored human mongrels . . .

"Whereas, It has been clearly demonstrated for the past twenty-five years or more that this plot cannot be defeated by small-men and small-women candidates for political office who, for fear of economic and political reprisal, neglect to expose the Communist-Jewish Conspiracy, yet run around shaking hands, babbling platitudes, and gabbing, ridiculous, exaggerated, fatuous and futile promises of luxury and security for our old people, money for our small farmers in distress, money and jobs for our unemployed, more money for our school teachers, more and better schools for our children, medical assistance for all, and—*less taxes*.

"Now, Therefore, I, John G. Crommelin . . . have filed . . ." etc [84]

Admiral Crommelin's candidacy was applauded not only by *Closer Up*, but also by *Right, Task Force, The Virginian*, and a great many other rightist periodicals His characterization of the Communist Conspiracy as Jewish has thoroughly established itself by now in the literature of most White Citizens Councils where it is graphically illustrated with names and photographs, and traced from the NAACP back through a maze of atom spies, international bankers, Big Dealers, Fair Dealers, New Dealers, to the Protocols of the Elders of Zion. One may procure from the Ku Klux Klan and other anti-integration agencies, photocopies of the official budget of the American Jewish Committee for 1953 which reveals that organization's expenditures for education on minority problems. Clearly, whatever funds were allocated have not been sufficient for this purpose! Presumably one could also procure a copy of this document from the American Jewish Committee itself, but in that case it would lack the explanatory introduction by Senator William E. Jenner.

It is the considered opinion of workers in the Anti-Defamation League that this material is used cynically by right wingers as a kind of political cement to bind together the various ill-assorted factions of their movement. But from long acquaintance with these fabrications, some of which are used over and over again to cover new situations that arise through the years, one comes to feel that many of those who distribute them have an absolute belief in their validity, and an almost mystical dependence on this whole idea of conspiracy to account for the miserable state of the world. Some of those who express the greatest fear of this conspiracy advocate a conspiratory atmosphere themselves. They recommend adopting "the enemys methods" (Americans Underground); seek an elite who will sign such a pledge as "I have never been a Communist, New Dealer, Fair Dealer" (Abraham Lincoln National Republican Club), or even "I hereby renounce any and all political allegiance to any and all other political parties and persons and henceforth, give my full political support to you until you die or resign" (Christian Anti-Jewish Party); use a kind of special language familar only to the initiate (*Grass Roots*); describe their personal persecutions by the "kept press" (Dan Smoot, Dec. 31, 1956); offer you private channels for receiving secret documents (*Aryan Views*), shops for securing Burnt Books (Adelaid Hering), augury, prophecy, divination (*Beacon News Herald*), and "inside" information on the coming Apocolypse (*Revere*). Characteristic of this call to conspiracy is a piece in F. Allen Mann's *Revere*, signed George Thomas Adams:

"Are you afraid to die? Or would you rather continue to live in a Communist-dominated country?

"In the coming months, many cesspools[85] of Communist subversion will be dynamited, crosses will be burned before the homes of professional Communist revolutionaries, and prisoners of communist treachery will be rescued from jails.

"These activities require men of courage, men such as those who threw the English tea into Boston Harbor, lynched Tories in Virginia, rammed bayonets into the bodies of hired soldiers sent here to destroy freedom. Luckily, the times are with us. This is a ripe period for those of us who have been driven to the point of desperation by Communist persecution. Suffering under an administration whose secret police harass patriots every day, an administration which applauded the slaughter of the Hungarian patriots, an administration whose sole purpose is that we shall live and die under Communism, what choice is left to us? Our blood is not so dear that it cannot be

shed in the cause of freedom. Let us be dead patriots rather than
live slaves. We shall not die in vain." [86]

One can imagine Bertrand Russell's confusion when he reads *this*
account of our police state and learns that the police persecute the
rightist rather than the communist; also when he finds Sidney Hook
agreeing with George Thomas Adams: "Whoever proclaims that life
is worth living under any circumstances has already written for himself an epitaph of infamy." [87]

Many of those quoted have thus identified Communism with the
Invisible Government, though not all have made it clear what purpose
lies behind the machinations of this conspiracy. Does it seek to
destroy civilization for its own pleasure? For revenge? For power?
But it already has all the power. Others, however, make it abundantly
clear that the conspiracy is the present incarnation of Satan and that
it is waging the devil's own battle—has indeed, never done anything
else since the beginning of the world. "Bible believers know that only
Christ himself can and shall someday stop this 'Satanic One World
Movement'," declares the *Alarming Cry*.[88]

To quote Joseph Stephen Kimmel, Iowa industrialist, board member
of the Campaign for 48 States, Patriotic Education, Inc., Committee for
Constitutional Government, and Defenders of the American Constitution:

"I firmly believe in God Almighty and the Holy Trinity as written
in the King James version of the Holy Bible.

"I firmly believe in the destiny of the American people as outlined
by the Declaration of Independence promulgated July 4, 1776, and the
American Constitution given forth September 17, 1787, as God-inspired
and for the betterment of the Human race.

"I firmly believe that the activities of the Communists internation-
ally and including the related insidious American machinations are
inspired of the devil in the never-ending strife of good and evil, and
that the present war against God and man is the all-out effort, using
all means military and other, including deceit, corruption, moral
disintegration and inhuman treatment of men, women and children,
*and as such must be resisted with all means within our power and on
no other basis*, whatever this involves." [89]

And Gerald L. K. Smith: "We have given our lives in resistance
to those satanic forces of the anti-Christ which seek to destroy this
Christian civilization root and branch. The same evil forces and the
same evil attributes of man which nailed Him to the cross and which
inspired the slaughtering techniques of Herod are now bent on the

destruction of our magnificent traditions as they relate to our nation, our world, and our personal lives." [90]

In the same terms Russell Maguire in *Planned Events* presents "seemingly unrelated events in many fields which confirm the enormity and complexity of the insidious pattern of the years gone by." In *Come to the Cross,* he explains further. "Evil forces within our borders have brainwashed us to turn to government seeking security, freedom, liberty and happiness. Our wise and succesful ancestors turned to God ... World Government is the Beast who will lead us to destruction. It will command that we bow down and worship the coming anti-Christ." So Dr. Lindsey finds the United Nations, dominated by Communists, as "Satanic in its origin," and so J. B. Matthews sees the Soviet Union as Satan at the summit conference.[91]

Once Satanism has moved from its original position in the ancient conspiracy to a more open seat in Communism, it is easy enough to identify it with what conservatives like to call the Liberal Establishment. As Andrew Lytle tells us, "Liberal democracy is part of the Christian drama, but it represents the devil. Liberty and fraternity are Christian words ... But equality exists nowhere in nature or society, nor indeed in the promise of afterlife. It is a word of false illusions, which is the devil's strategy." [92]

Or as *Right* has it: "The fight for the Right; for nationalism, individualism and the Christian tradition, and against internationalism, collectivism, and off-brand religions, is really a fight for survival and a fight to the finish. Let the Right understand, and fearlessly proclaim to the world that liberalism is treason." [93]

Liberalism, then, is Satanism, and, according to *Right,* treason. This double identification has been largely accepted by the Congressional committees which have investigated American Communism, and certainly by J. Edgar Hoover in most of his speeches and publications, though there is some tendency to soften the accusation by referring to liberals as dupes rather than traitors, or else as pseudo-liberals. Actually there seems to be no more reason for calling these people, who are sufficiently named and placed, pseudo-liberals, than for speaking of right-wingers as pseudo-conservatives. They include all those who were in any way identified with the New Deal, unless they have broken with it and proved willing to testify against it in the manner of Raymond Moley, John T. Flynn, John Dos Passos, and Donald Richberg. Their twenty years of treason have been endlessly chronicled, most recently by Robert Morris, former counsel for the Senate Internal Security Subcommittee, who lists Adlai Stevenson and Dean Acheson among "the fools (and worse) who have made Communist triumphs possible." The hard core of the Right Wing is willing to add the names of the Eisenhower brothers to this list, and those of the Palace Guard, and in fact seems to place the names of Wendell Willkie, Paul Hoffman, and Eric Johnston almost as high as those of Franklin Roosevelt and Harry Truman. As Ida Darden says in the *Southern Conservative*: "When we take care of the domestic home-grown variety of Communists clustered in Washington, in the colleges, universities, churches, on the lecture platforms and in other strategic places in this country, we will have International Communism licked and not before." [94]

It has been customary for educated people to attribute all this talk to the usual ill-mannered tradition of American political debate, and to see little more than a vivid metaphor in the right wing references to satanic powers and dark forces moving us, like paws in a game, towards national destruction. This attitude is probably as mistaken as the more hostile one which can only deflate and ridicule. It should be obvious that a great many conservative writers and readers believe absolutely that this country is in the grip of a savage, ruthless, and even supernatural conspiracy; that disciplined known men, not abstract nouns, are the foreign agents of this conspiracy, and that these agents, under specific directives from their masters, control every single key point in American life and policy.

Nor is this belief by any means limited to irresponsible and unofficial spokesmen for the Right. In Courtney Whitney's authoritative biography of Gen. Douglas MacArthur, the matter is plainly put: "MacArthur understood. He had long been helplessly aware that even his top-secret dispatches to Washington came under the scrutiny of unauthorized persons ... It was almost as if the highest officials there were conspiring against him. It would not be long before MacArthur would discover that in fact, they were." [95]

Battle Line, an official publication of the Republican National Committee, commenting on former Secretary of State Dean Acheson's press statement that the "very serious situation" facing America "is due as much to the inaction of the [Eisenhower] Administration as to Soviet actions," had this to say: "This is the same Dean Acheson who held top posts in the State Department during the year when 600 million people fell under the yoke of Communism. This is the same man who set the China policy of waiting until the dust settled. This is the same man who put Korea outside of the United States defense perimeter. And this is the same Dean Acheson who said he would never turn his back on Alger Hiss. Today the nation is reaping the harvest of those seeds sowed by Acheson." The seeds referred to are *The Seeds of Treason* described by Ralph DeToledano and Victor Lasky in the book of that name, an account of the trial of Alger Hiss.⁹⁶

The name of Hiss serves as a sort of open sesame to many revelations of the same kind. Consider William Buckley's telegram to critics, commentators and news analysists on the publication of Mr. Hiss' *In the Court of Public Opinion* in May, 1957: "Analyzed from the standpoint of Bolshevik tactical methods, what do you believe to be the primary political objective sought by the appearance of the Alger Hiss Book at this time?" Hiss, in other words, is assumed to have no personal motivations, but to act only on orders. He is an actual foreign agent and a marionette, operated by wires that become more clearly visible as time passes and the light is let in.⁹⁷

Add the editorials in the *Saturday Evening Post* and the *American Legion Magazine*. Add the committee reports of the House un-American Activities Committee and the Senate Internal Security Subcommittee, and the books, articles, and speeches of J. Edgar Hoover, Robert Morris, John Bricker, Richard Arens, Francis E. Walter, Richard Nixon, William Knowland, Robert Stripling, William E. Jenner, Barry Goldwater, James Eastland, Eugene Talmadge, Gordon Scherer, Ralph Gwinn, George W. Malone, Karl Mundt, Everett Dirksen, Noah Mason, Usher L. Burdick, Henry C. Dworshak, Styles Bridges, Carroll B. Reece, Andrew Schoeppel, Andrew Langer, J. Bracken Lee, to say nothing of Joseph McCarthy. These men, and many others, are all honored as freedom fighters by the Right, where it is believed that without them the fifth column would have prevailed long ago. (*Fifth amendment* is clearly associated in the popular mind with *fifth column*.)

One is particularly struck by the devotion to this end of Robert E. Stripling and Robert O. Morris, each of whom might well be described by William Rusher's comment on Morris: "Dedicated ... Deeply informed, constantly vigilant, utterly tireless, he prodded overworked and often timid Senators into a regimen of legislative hearings that kept a substantial part of America's Communists breathless, frightened, and impotent." These men are true believers of the Right, and appear to deserve far more of the credit for our wars with the conspiracy than do the congressmen they assisted. Morris recently ran for Governor of New Jersey and Stripling is canvassing his native state of Texas as an agent of Freedom in Action, a group devoted to "vigilant Constitutional patriotism," "to fortify citizen-meetings with usable facts." Neither one has given up the good fight.[98]

It might be pointed out here at the risk of being obvious that even the most rabid anti-communists of the Left do not seem to share this conception of communism in America as a formation of men, all of whom can be pinpointed with time, patience, and cooperative witnesses, and eventually defrocked, deported or destroyed. They think rather of a system of ideas which has affected the thinking of all mankind, and which they believe must be countered with saner philosophy. If the men harboring these ideas are citizens of the United States, and not actual foreign agents, then of course they cannot be punished for their way of thinking.[99]

There is a very real, and not merely a political, difference of opinion here, and one that will hardly be resolved by name-calling. On the Left, furthermore, there is often a feeling that the government of the USSR, dictatorship though it is, represents the Russian people and is preferred by them to the czarist regime that preceded it. It seems clear to leftists that this government is not going to disappear, and that the United States must manage in some fashion to coexist with it. And it is hoped that discussions in the United Nations and elsewhere will eventually bring about some *modus vivendi* which is workable for both countries. That they have been disappointed in these hopes time after time does not alter the fact that no other method of procedure seems to present itself to their minds. Some, indeed, go farther, and declare that we have made no single approach to the Soviets at any time which could possibly be accepted by them as in their interest, and that whatever overtures we did make were always accompanied by such expressions of distrust and dismay from the Right that the Russians were possibly justified in believing that they were not made with the acceptance of the American people, as indeed, perhaps they were not. They are not impressed by the list of broken Russian promises which the Right is always repeating, asserting that some were not promised and that others were differently understood.[100]

Rightists, on the other hand, feel that *any* association with the Soviet government is appeasement, and betrayal of the Russian people who are thought to be held in bondage by a little band of gangsters. They feel it is our bounden duty to withdraw recognition from this kangaroo government, both in the United States and the United Nations (if that institution is to be allowed to persist), and to give every encouragement and assistance short of war to the enslaved people, who are on the verge of revolt, and will overthrow their dicta-

tors if we outlaw them. Up to the present time this has been the
official position of both Dean Acheson and John Foster Dulles, despite
the fact that no Rightist can see this, and if any relaxation seems to
be developing, it can only be based on a revised estimate of Russian
strength.[101] Rightists observe frequently that we cannot do business
with dictators, and reflect that the present attitude of the Left was
reversed exactly in the cases of Franco Spain and Nazi Germany,
and that it was the Left which then looked for foreign agents, conspiracy and sedition among the writers of the Right.[102] It can be added
the present attitude of the Right was reversed in those days, too.

IV

These same patterns of thought are, of course, extended to the Far
East and the Middle East. And here it is curious to observe that the
anti-foreign Right has a deep and lasting attachment to the Nationalist Chinese government of Chiang Kai-shek, and has a strong paternal
interest in the affairs of Egypt's Gamal Nasser. Both of these men,
though known to be dictators, are thought of as dictators that we
can do business with, and as our first line of defense against communism abroad; and it is held with some bitterness that we have
treacherously betrayed the one and will presently betray the other.
Freda Utley, in *The China Story,* and more recently in *Will the Middle
East Go West?* has made a great effort to enlist support for this position.[108]

More useful, perhaps, in approaching the China tangle is Herbert
Feis's book of that name, and the analysis of H. Bradford Westerfield.
Westerfiield explains the "orientalism" of conservatives as resulting
from their long-established relations with China, first through the rich
China trade, then through the activities of American missionaries,
teachers, and medical men; through the historical connection of Republican presidents, especially McKinley and Theodore Roosevelt,
with critical periods of American-Pacific relations; through admiration
for Douglas MacArthur, dating from the time he was Hoover's Chief
of Staff and put down the bonus marchers; and finally from the persis-
tent feeling during World War II that the war in the Pacific was "their
war." Because no bipartisan policy was set up for postwar relations
with China, as was carefully and successfully done in regard to
Europe, it appeared to most Republicans that the shocking loss of their
beloved China to the Communists was entirely the fault of the
Democratic foreign policy; though actually, he says, the Democrats

had established no policy at all, but had left the whole matter to the routine operations of the Far Eastern division of the State Department.[104]

Westerfield charges the China hands in the Far Eastern Division with "an extreme missionary humanitarianism" at a time when their attention should have been given to "the realities of power politics." The "influence of the far leftist opinion in and out of the Department of State" he finds "obscure but perhaps important." This is an extremely cautious interpretation from a conservative writer, and one that most rightists would instantly brand as communist-inspired, because on no issue have most rightists been more indefatigable than in their efforts to stamp out the virulent communist infection in the Far Eastern Division.[105]

The whole fantastic story of the Division, of *Amerasia,* the Institute of Pacific Relations, and Senator McCarthy's announcement that Owen Lattimore was the chief architect of our foreign policy in the Far East as well as top espionage agent for the Soviets in the United States, has largely disappeared from the popular press, as one after another of its protagonists have received judicial clearance. But not for a moment have the fires stopped burning on the Right. From the China Lobby to the Committee of Endorsers, from the Fighting Homefolks of Fighting Men to the Committee of One Million Against the Admission of Red China, from the Congress of Freedom to the Christian Crusader, there is still hope of bringing the great Christian Generalissimo back from Formosa to govern the Chinese mainland. We must on no account compound our earlier desertion of Chiang by recognition of Red China, according to these groups, and to admit this imposter to the United Nations will make it impossible for the Nationalists ever to "liberate their country from the satanic hold of the Communists," as Billy Hargis puts it in "Help 'Bomb' Red China!' Reverend Hargis is planning to flood Red China with hydrogen-filled balloons carrying "the plan of salvation printed in the Chinese language." [106]

Rightist enthusiasm for Gamal Nasser is less widespread than for Chiang, but it is equally intense in some quarters. There is no tradition of support for Egypt or the Arabs generally, but one is developing as the Arab League distributes its literature to rightist groups and is much quoted. It is felt that intelligent support from the United States will keep the Arabs from going communist, and in fact many writers on the Left have joined in this proposition, and for more countries than Egypt. The significant fact about Nasser for many rightists, however, is his hostility to Israel, and despite all the evidence of his many links with Soviet Russia, it is frequently believed that this hostility is a clear indication of his anti-communism.[107]

The old identification of the Invisible Government with the Jewish Communist conspiracy and Satanism frequently underlies such thinking, and though some rightists such as Freda Utley protest that they have nothing of the sort in mind, there is no doubt that they call it to mind for many of their readers. This is not to say, as spokesman for the Anti-Defamation League sometimes appear to be saying, that anti-Zionism is anti-Semitism.[108] Many thoughtful Jews and non-Jews who applaud the establishment of Israel have found fault on occasion with its government.

Rightists, of course, see in Zionism another alarming combination of internationalism and collectivism—of foreigners with a centralized organization—and are inclined to look upon Jewish organizations (as distinguished from their Jewish friends) as another fifth column in America, fostering "dual citizenship," and other suspicious deviations. Such people are determined to see Israel as an outpost of Soviet Russia, and the American Jew as its agent, and they seem unable to grasp the contradictions involved in this assumption. The idea is encouraged of course, by Arab apologists.[109]

An interesting summary of the modern American anti-Jewish position and its relation to Israel appears in Merwin K. Hart's *Economic Council Letter*.[110] Hart says firmly that American Jews are entitled to all the rights to which other Americans are entitled, but then he makes clear that he feels that they are *not* entitled (in official groups) to work for desegregation, civil rights legislation, changes in the immigration law, the defeat of conservative political candidates, assistance for the state of Israel, separation of church and state in public education, dilution of Christianity by brotherhood movements of Christians and Jews, or world government —especially world government which "would include Israel, and would be guided by the 'ethics' of Israel." He clearly feels that all Jews, whether working publicly in organized groups or privately as individuals, belong to a closed international corporation which operated with the communists "to mold the American Republic into something very different from what it has always been"—in fact, to make it subject to a world government. It is no wonder that Jewish right wingers such as Isaac Don Levine have difficulty in admiring Hart. Hart's *Economic Council Letter* is often reprinted in the *Congressional*

Record, and representatives of the Council frequently testify before Congressional Committees.

The inter-relation of right-wing interests has been traced here at some length because these interests characteristically occur together in the works of right-wing writers. Observe that there is one dominant image which particularly identifies right-wing thinking. This is the concept of the enslaved people dominated by corrupt leaders. The Right constantly appeals to these people to throw off the yoke and become free men. Or it will warn them that if they don't muzzle their leaders, others will have to do it for them, and then all will suffer. The people of the Iron Curtain Countries, for example, and of Soviet Russia and Red China, must rebel against the tyrants of the Communist party. The rank and file of labor must rebel against the gangsters and demagogues who hold them in thrall. The Jews of America must put down the "leading Jews." The American Negroes must rise up against the NAACP. The Christians must throttle the internationalists who run the National Council of Churches. Responsible educators must deflate the NEA. And all of us must unite to tie the hands of the Supreme Court, the Federal Government, and above all, the United Nations.

There is rarely any recognition from the Right that some of these leaders may possibly be attempting to serve the real interests of those who gave them power, nor any apparent realization of the practical difficulties encountered in activating any program. It seems almost as if the Right were opposed to leadership in its very nature, to any sort of organization sufficiently powerful to generate pressure, and in fact to any person or group in a position to cope with public affairs instead of theorizing about how they should be handled. This general tendency has led some commentators to describe right wingers as anarachists rather than conservatives.

In summary, the American Right Wing may be said to include all those who share the conviction that the relationship of government to the individual should be severely limited. In the literature of the movement, specific limitations are systematically proposed in the name of anti-federalism and anti-internationalism. Right wingers would limit the taxing and spending powers of Congress, balance the budget at whatever cost, and stabilize present fluid procedures in the Federal Reserve Bank and the United States Treasury. They ask the complete withdrawal of government from the regulation of industry, from labor-management relations, from public utilities, from business enterprise in any field. They desire to outlaw full employment in industry, collective bargaining, the closed shop, and political education for union members. They ask the complete withdrawal of government from the supervision of health, education and welfare, and the immediate voiding of all programs dealing with social security, medical insurance, fluoridation, polio vaccine, mental health, cultural development, adult education, and federal aid to schools. They desire a redistribution of Congressional powers to the state legislatures and of judicial powers from the federal to the state courts. And they call for the prosecution of ministers who preach the social gospel, and of teachers who recommend social planning, as communists and traitors.

In the international field, right wingers seek to limit the power of the president to make treaties, and the power of the State Department to issue visas and passports. They would put an immediate end to foreign aid, and to the participation of the United States in the United Nations, UNESCO, NATO, GATT, ILO, and any remaining Point Four Programs of Technical Assistance. They would withdraw recognition from the USSR, Israel, and most Iron Curtain countries, and close the door to any communication with these countries or with Red China. They would ask the UN to meet elsewhere and immediately raze the building. They would further reduce the limited immigration allowed by the McCarran-Walter Law, make full use of deportation, denaturalization and repatriation, and establish a kind of provisional citizenship for Negros, Zionists, liberals, and all those whose families were naturalized less than two generations ago. And finally, they would give full rein to Congressional investigating commitees to check on these and all other matters, and confidently place the resulting prosecutions in the hands of the Justice Department.

One would suppose that even the most dedicated right winger would recognize the utopian quality of these proposals in their totality, and foresee the paralysis of the country that would follow their adoption. And certainly it is true that though they are frequently incorporated into bills, they rarely become law without extensive alteration. But it appears that the real strength of the Right lies in the very abstractness of its most cherished dogmas, so that a leftist must go considerably more than halfway to make a balanced compromise with the Right in any matter of action. Or to state it another way, when so many Americans are committed to so conservative a program, there is bound to be considerable attrition, and any sharply-honed new idea is likely to be considerably dulled by the constant friction of an older one.

In pursuing this metaphor, one notes again that right wingers keep in constant touch with their Congressmen—write letters, send telegrams, mail reprints of articles, testify before committees, and are often quoted in the *Congressional Record*. Their papers are lively chronicles of the bills that are up before each house, and they keep a vigilant eye on all legislative matters. Today there is no comparable body of political writing from the left, except for the trade union papers, which are less in volume and more limited in coverage.

The result has been a conservative government in the Eisenhower years and a paralyzed government in Kennedy's first year.

As of November, 1961, it is clear that events have moved rapidly in directions that are consistent with the previous doctrines, beliefs and actions of the American Right Wing.

Between the Spring of 1958 and the Fall of 1961, there has been increasing tension on all the issues that worry the American Right Wing, as well as many other segments of the American public. As the Right Wingers see the current scene:

On the domestic scene, the economy seemed unable to recover, without external stimulation, sufficiently to keep unemployment down to acceptable levels. The importation of "cheap" foreign products caused distress in some domestic industries. Evidences of graft and corruption in the Federal projects that did get underway (for example in the Federal Highway Construction program in New Mexico and elsewhere) were of sufficient magnitude to give States Righters new ammunition for their battles.

The segregation issue in the schools has not quieted down and has hardened feelings of hatred between races and toward the Federal Government, including the Supreme Court.

Pressure for increased medical care for the aged, generated during the 1960 election, has enlarged the scope of the fight against "socialized medicine."

The sudden shifting attitude of the public towards the public schools has gone in directions that coincide with the wishes of the American Right Wing and has thus given them a legitimate reason for hunting out the educators they claimed all along were imposing subversive doctrines in the schools.

Exposure of corruption in the police departments of Chicago, Denver and elsewhere, the fines imposed on General Electric officials for price fixing and Congressional hearings on the drug industry bringing to light evidences of excess profiteering, plus widespread evidences of juvenile deliquency, have been cited as evidences that our society is sick and that the sickness resulted from our abandonment of old-fashioned doctrines of Americanism.

The Right Wing's claims that the influence of the communists in our midst has been increasing was dramatized by the film "Operation Abolition", which has been shown in all parts of the land.

The heat generated during the 1960 election over the church and state issue carried over into the fight in Congress for Federal aid to schools, an issue that has now become deeply engrained in the consciousness of the public and has aroused the Right Wing and others, to an all out battle to keep education under local control.

Fear of organized labor has quickened with the prospect that Hoffa may extend his power, and by the charges that Reuther exercises great power over the Kennedy Administration.

The Right Wing's general distrust of the Federal Government has been intensified by the appointment to positions of responsibility of men they considered dangerous, if not actually disloyal—Schlesinger, Stevenson, Governor Williams, and Bowles, for example.

Again, as they see things, *on the international scene,* the worst fears of the Right Wing have been realized. The Russians now have a base just a few miles from our shores and may control most of Latin and South America. The Government's abortive invasion of Cuba demonstrated its lack of comprehension of the nature of the danger and its lack of "guts".

That our expenditure of billions of dollars on foreign aid has won us no friends and has at the same time weakened our economy seriously, as was feared by the Right Wing, has been proven to their satisfaction. At the same time Russia, without great expenditures of dollars, seems to have no trouble in recruiting uncommitted nations to their side. We seem to have no success in waging psychological warfare.

Russia's progress in space science and in expanding their own industrial might, while we waste our resources on the production of luxury goods, points clearly to the time when we will be the weaker of the two nations and thus will be conquered.

France's internal struggles cast doubt on the ability of the NATO powers to hold together, while the course of events in Berlin increases the gnawing fear that West Germany will fall under Russian influence.

Russia's ability to create crises where and when she wishes, places us on the defensive and keeps us running all over the globe to put out fires (and to waste our resources) wherever she starts them.

Uncertainty as to what the true relations of China and Russia are fans the fear that the dilemmas we now face are mere peanuts in comparison with what the China issue will be when and if Russia decides to loose it upon us.

And while we and other nations appear about to batter one another to complete destruction, Israel increases in strength and stability and prepares to occupy the role the Right Wing has consistently predicted—the one nation that will triumph and will rule all—the great international conspiracy.

Russia's attempts to paralyze the United Nations over the question of the nature of the Secretariatship offers the Right Wing more evidence for their belief that we should not be a part of this, or other, international organizations.

When it is realized that the Right Wing has predicted these disasters and outcomes—both domestic and international—it is not surprising that during the last three years the Right Wing has expanded its influence and membership. It can claim that had its warnings been heeded and its doctrines accepted, these disasters would not have occurred.

Prior to 1961 the Right Wing organizations and influence were unorganized, scattered and often working at cross purposes and without central leadership. But, as the dangers increased and the crises deepened, it was inevitable that all these forces would begin to pull together and to find central direction and leadership that would gradually acquire political potency.

Two poles of central forces have developed around Senator Barry Goldwater and Robert Welch and the John Birch Society. The progress of this coalescing has been documented, described and evaluated in several recent books and articles.[111]

As for what the Right Wing has been saying during the past few years there is little that is new or different from what had been said previously.

In terms of new forms of action, one can cite the work of the John Birch Society in carrying on an essay contest to arouse interest in the impeachment of Justice Warren. And, although precise documentation is probably impossible, it is obvious that the Society is beginning to be able to exert considerable influence at the local level all over the country. No longer can it be said that Right Wingers are "crackpots". The John Birch Society chapters include respectable community leaders and solid citizens who feel that the basic doctrines, if not the fringe issues, of the Right Wing coincide with their own.

On the campuses of the universities, there are now ultra-conservative organizations, containing both students and faculty, such as the Forum for Young Americans.

The influence of the John Birch Society on the government has been felt in many ways. In her *Distaff* syndicated column that appeared during the week of October 16, 1961, Doris Fleeson cites the success the Society has had in forcing a Senate Sub-Committee to make a "frank" analysis of the role of the Pentagon in the case of Major General Edwin A. Walker. But this is of little importance in comparison with the limitations the Right Wing has placed around President Kennedy in his handling of the Berlin crisis. Walter Lippmann, in his columns published during September and early October, 1961, has documented these limitations thoroughly.

It has not been the intent or purpose of this report to pass judgment on the American Right Wing movement, but only to describe it accurately and to document it so that historians of the future will be able to evaluate its role. Each person's stand on the issues involved will determine his attitude toward the point of view and actions of the Right Wing.

Ten years ago, liberals, moderates and uncommitted citizens could, and did, scoff at the Right Wing as a "fringe" group concerned in a crazy manner with unimportant issues. What they failed to understand, and what this report tries to clarify, is the fact that in terms of basic economic, political, social and governmental issues the Right Wing held the same beliefs as did the moderate conservatives of both major parties. They differed only in their concern with fringe issues, in their manner of speaking and in their sense of fair play.

The significance of recent developments is simply that in a time of deep crisis, the moderates are more willing to go along with, and be carried by, the extremists.

The question raised by these trends is whether or not they will lead to a pattern set by Italy or Germany, or whether we will, as we did in the 1920's when the K. K. K. spread over the land, return to our previous adherence to moderation and sense of fair play.

It would be a rash man, indeed, who could predict the outcome of the current struggle to determine the character and political complexion of this nation.

REFERENCES

1. In this paper the term *right* is used very simply as opposed to *left*, and the entire political spectrum is considered as divided between the two. Many gradations are distinguished within each division, but none ouside. This is the usual schema used by right wing writers, not always recognized by them as arbitrary.

2. See Wilbur H. Baldinger, "Reading From the Right," and "Marching Orders For the Political Right," *The Progressive*, June, 1956 and February, 1957; John Roy Carlson, *Under Cover* and *The Plotters*, New York, Dutton, 1943, 1946; Benjamin R. Epstein and Arnold Foster, *The Troublemakers* and *Cross-Currents*, Garden City, New York, Doubleday, 1952, 1956; Gordon Hall, *The Hate Campaign Against the UN*, Boston, Beacon, 1952; *Neo-Fascist and Hate Groups*, Report of the UN-American Activities Committee, Dec. 17, 1954; E. A. Pillar, *Time Bomb*, New York, Arco, 1945; "Radical Reactionaries," *The Progressive*, December, 1953; Ralph Lord Roy, *Apostles of Discord*, Boston, Beacon, 1953; *Subversive Activities of Hate Groups*, Report of the Americanism Commission, American Legion, Department of Illinois. See also Rexford G. Tugwell, *The Democratic Roosevelt*, Garden City, New York, Doubleday, 1957, p. 429.

3. See Daniel Bell, *The New American Right*, New York, Criterion, 1955, and Esmond Wright, "Radicals of the Right," *Political Quarterly*, XXVII, 4, pp. 366-377. Clinton Rossiter, *Conservatism in America*, New York, Knopf, 1955, distinguishes a small group of extremists (less than 5% of the American Right) from other conservatives, but it appears that on political issues their differences are much less significant than their likenesses. See also Rossiter's article in *Harper's*, April 1957, and cf. Sidney Hook, "The New Conservatism," *The New Leader*, July 8, 1957, and Cushing Stout, "Liberalism, Conservatism and the Babel of Tongues," *Partisan Review*, Winter 1958.

4. Bell, *op. cit.*, p. 16 and *passim*, esp. p. 217: "It is extremely doubtful that the radical right will grow beyond the peak of 1953-54."

5. William Stephenson, editor of *The Virginian*, in a letter of June 12, 1957.

6. Most of these are listed in *The First National Directory of "Rightist" Groups, Publications and some Individuals in the United States (and Some Foreign Countries)*, 3d ed., San Francisco, Liberty and Property, 1957. The State University of Iowa Library has an extensive collection of the publications of these groups, many of them received as gifts from the publishers, and other contributed by various congressmen as characteristic of the bulk of Congressional mail.

7. George Racey Jordan, former president of the American Coalition of New York, in a personal letter. Dan Smoot reports that he has 5,000 paid subscribers, *Right* 3,000, *Human Events* (in January 1957) 28,400—more than either the *Nation* or the *New Republic*. The Intercollegiate Society of Individualists says it had 7,000 students enrolled in 1957. *National Review* (October 11, 1958, p. 255) claims an average of 19,080 copies distributed each issue.

8. John Hitchings sees "the number of US patriots" increasing, "due to the stupidity of the enemy in declaring war on the South." Writing from Southport, Florida, he says, "They now have a Citizens Council in this County, and I (formerly distrusted as a Yankee) am feeding them material and trying to arrange for Hugh Grant to address them." (*Free Enterprise*, August 14, 1956, p. 3.) Hitchings organized a Buy

47

American Campaign to boycott the wares of leftist firms. He is the Southwestern Director of We the People. Cf. Hugh Grant's address to the Florida Federation for Constitutional Government, March 13, 1958, distributed by the *Georgia Tribune*: "The United States of America at the Crossroads: Which Road America?"

9. W. E. Michael's "Tragedy of Errors" about Kasper and Clinton was read into the *Congressional Record* by Senator Russell; reprints were distributed by the Tennessee Federation.

10. *National Review*, March 8, 1958, p. 236.

11. See *Women's Voice*, September 1957, p. 2: "We the People's Convention . . . can be summed up in Don Bell's words: Apple pies but no apples . . . The deadly head of the Corba is at the throat of our country, but the program dealt only with some harmless little garter snakes." And on p. 7: "For the benefit of Patriots who were bitterly disappointed at the results of the 'We, the People' Convention, *Women's Voice* held a Constitution Day Rally at the Atlantic Hotel." Among the speakers, in addition to Mrs. Lyrl Clarke Van Hyning, editor of *Women's Voice*, were Agnes Waters, Elizabeth Dilling, and William Stephenson. See also *Free Enterprise*, November 15, 1956, for an account by Harry T. Everingham of the dispute within We the People over the third party issue.

12. The American Legion, Department of California, was outraged at the suggestion that its campaign against UNESCO was organized by Smith. See *Analysis of the Ray Murphy Committee Report*, Americanism Commission, Department of Texas, American Legion, Houston, 1955. Fulton Lewis, Jr. told Mike Wallace in a televised interview on February 1, 1958, that Smith was not allowed in his office. Richard Nixon denounced him. Smith reports all this quite philosophically, but regrets the hypocrisy of it. See *The Cross and the Flag*, March 1958, pp. 3-4, and July 1958, p. 14.

13. The Bar Association did not distribute or officially approve the 1957 report of its Committee on Communist Tactics, Strategy and Objectives concerning the Supreme Court's "aid and comfort to the enemy," but it is available from many right wingers. Copies may be purchased from Mrs. Phyllis Schlafly, Alton, Illinois. See note 69. See also Report for 1958 in the *Congressional Record*, August 22, 1958, p. 17,717. Gordon Hall in his *Hate Campaign Against the UN* would separate such groups as the American Bar Association, the D.A.R. and the Legion from his discussion of the rest. but it is difficult to see on what basis. Resolutions adopted by the D.A.R. for example, on April 17, 1958, are purest right wing doctrine, as appears clearly enough in the approving summary in *Women's Voice*, May 1958, p. 1:

"The D.A.R. ending their 67th continental congress April 17, 1958, have justified their heritage. They approved resolutions urging that the United States withdraw from the U.N. and break diplomatic relations with Russia. They also urged that the U.N. headquarters be moved out of this country. They condemned mixed racial marriages as a 'communist objective' and opposed the 'political and socialistic one-world activities of the National Council of Churches of Christ in America'; they passed resolutions against reciprocal trade agreements and any merger of the armed forces into a single service with a single chief of staff. They reaffirmed a stand against any federal aid to education and suggested strengthening schools and colleges at local and state levels. Last but not least they took a positive and forthright stand against water fluoridation."

One is, however, reminded by analogy that liberal publications have frequently and fairly objected that because their aims coincided with those of the *Daily Worker*, they were not, for that reason, to be called Communist. Yet neither they nor the *Worker* would probably object to being called *Left*, as opposed to *Right*. Rightist groups exhibit as many differences as do leftist groups, but we are chiefly concerned here with likenesses. *Human Events* (June 8, 1957, p. 1) claims that right wingers make up 90 per cent of the GOP. Fulton Lewis, Jr. in a Mike Wallace interview (February 1, 1958) said he believed that 75% of the people in the U.S. are conservatives. Seymour M. Lipset in *The New American Right, op. cit.*, pp. 228-229, finds that non-voting Americans are even more conservative than those who go to the polls. (One reads often in rightist papers that it is little use to vote for either party, since both are identically liberal.)

14. *Right*, January 1958, p. 1, and August 1957, p. 1. If the Liberty Lobby or the Survival Commission should make any great headway, it will probably become known as a conspiracy. It has been easy for alarmists to view the Right Wing as ruthless, organized conspiracy, and it has frequently been charged with all those evils which the Right now regularly attributes to the Left. Such writers as Carlson, Roy, Forster and Epstein speak of working under cover in such a movement, of interlocking directorates, and of sinister contacts with foreign dictators such as Franco, Nasser, and Germany's reviving Nazi clique.

In the famous Mass Sedition Trial of 1944 (see Maximilan St. George and Lawrence Dennis, *A Trail on Trial: the Great Sedition Trial of 1944*, National Civil Rights Committee, 1946) the government seems to have made the same simplification, expecting to find a secret network of treason and espionage where what actually existed was only an open, and in fact deafening, concert of interests and beliefs. These interests and beliefs have always seemed un-American to American progressives, and for the very good reason that many conservative writers do express constantly their desire to subvert and overthrow those achievements of government which are most dear to the progressives. There is sometimes violent talk among them of direct action, and their bitterness, acidity, vindictiveness, and despair have on occasion given a certain appropriateness to the term *hate-monger*. As unfair and ridiculous as these charges seem to the conservative, however, one must observe that it never occurs to him to see any analogy here to his own inflexible attitude toward the communist conspiracy.

15. Clinton Rossiter, *Conservatism in America*, and Richard Hofstadter, "The Revolt of the Pseudo-Conservatives" in *The New American Right* edited by Daniel Bell, are among those trying to preserve the etymological purity of word *conservative*. This is probably as hopeless as the efforts of English teachers to confine the meaning of the verb *transpire* to 'breathe.'

16. Archibald Roosevelt, director of The Alliance, in *Manual for American Action*, pp. 4-6. "We must learn to speak in the name of millions both loud and clear." The term *libertarian* also has some currency among conservatives who think of themselves as upholding individual liberty of thought and action, but in spite of excellent support for it from Dean Russell ("Who Is a Libertarian?" *Ideas on Liberty*, May 1955) and Verne Kaub ("Segregation Ruling Repeals Free Will," *The Virginian*, February 1956, p. 3), it has not gained wide acceptance. *Free Enterprise* published a "Libertarian Directory" in its issue for September 15, 1955. Cf. *Faith and Freedom*, June 1956, p. 8; George Peck in American Progress III, No. 1, p. 10; *The Character of a Nation*, Intercollegiate Society of Individualists' pamphlet, 1957, cover verso. One might say that there seems to be a kind of permanent and fruitful tension between the libertarians and the authoritarians in the movement. Note, incidentally, that the

publishers of the leftist journal *Dissent* speak of reasserting "the libertarian values of the socialist ideal."

17. An expression or metaphor will appear in one paper, and then suddenly occur in dozen of others. For example, this bit of gnomic wisdom was noted in the *Christian Beacon*, January 24, 1957: "Chickens come home to roost." Then in succession we have: "Chickens Come Home to Roost," *Closer Up*, March 27, 1957, p. 2; "their chickens are coming home to roost," *The Virginian*, March 1957, p. 3; Harry Elmer Barnes, "The Chickens of the Interventionist Liberals Have Come Home to Roost;" *Northwest Industrial News*, May 1957, p. 1, "The 'chickens are coming home to roost' at the University of Minnesota's College of Education;" *Grass Roots*, July 1957, "Chickens will come home to roost;" Bob Shuler quoted in *Right*, September 1957, "Chickens come home to roost;" *Free Enterprise*, September 1957, p. 1, "Ike's chickens come home to roost;" New Letter, Nov. 1, 1957 "Today However, in Boston, Chickens are Coming Home to Roost." Bulletin of the Council for Basic Education, January 1958, "We thought there was nobody here but us chickens. Since Sputnik, however . . . the roost is crowded"; Melchior Palyi, *Nineteen Hundred Fifty Eight*, December 30, 1957, "A majority of the chickens, hatched since 1933 by our foreign policy, will come home to roost." *Farm and Ranch Magazine*, January 1958, "The chickens—and the Sputniks—have come home to roost;" *Human Events*, May 12, 1958, " 'Built-in' wage increases have come home to roost."

18. Richard Whalen, "A Fresh Wind Will Blow," *U.S.A.*, January 3, 1958. See also Medford Evans, "Why I Am an Anti-Intellectual," and Styles Bridges, "Keep the Experts on 'Tap' but not on 'Top' " in *Human Events*, January 26 and October 19, 1957; "Grass Roots Rebels—Conservative Liberals," *Our Country*, January 1958; Anthony Harrigan, "Some Notes on American Conservatives" *U.S.A.*, April 26, 1953; William Henry Chamberlin, "The Evolution of a Conservative," *National Review*, April 12, 1958, pp. 349-350; Dwight MacDonald, *Memoirs of a Revolutionist*, New York, Farrar, 1957, p. 6; p. 333.

19. John Fischer, "Why Is the Conservative Voice So Hoarse?" *Harper's Magazine*, March 1956, p. 16. Fischer's characterization of the *National Review* as radical is sustained by members of the San Marino, California, Exchange Club who find it communistic and atheistic, according to Eric Pridonoff, *National Review*, June 7, 1958, p. 536. Kirk spoke at a Congress of Freedom meeting, April 17, 1958, in Kansas City, Missouri, where he may have improved his relations with the real working conservatives. His report (*National Review*, May 3, 1958) is a little patronizing. See John Chamberlain, "Stop-Loss Conservatives," *National Review*, May 4, 1957, "a whole stable of mildly collectivist Trojan Horses . . . have lodged in the libertarian camp."

20. Donald Davidson, *Tyranny at Oak Ridge*, published and distributed by the Tennessee Federation for Constitutional Government, Nashville, 1956. Davidson is chairman of the Federation. See tribute to him in the *National Review*, May 8, 1957, p. 550. John Crowe Ransom's *Poems and Essays* contains a gentlemanly review of Russell Kirk's *The Conservative Mind*.

21. "Pro-Communism in American Colleges," *Human Events*, March 23, 1957.

22. These names appear in many booklists distributed by right wing groups, such as *All-American Books*, a quarterly published by John T. Flynn's America's Future; the Freedom Booklist, distributed by the Freedom Club of Los Angeles; the *Do You Know* list, Houston, Texas, 1957; and Phyllis Schlafly's *Reading List for Americans*, 3d ed., Alton Illinois, 1958.

23. *The True Believer*, New York, Harper, 1951, p. 137.

24. Schlafly, *op. cit.*, p. 16. Cf. Frank L. Hughes, *Prejudice and the Press*, New York, Devin-Adair, 1950. The Freedom School has been recently opened in Colorado Springs with a libertarian program. Robert LeFevre is Director. Trilling, *The Liberal Imagination*, New York, Viking, 1950, p. ix. Lipsett, Martin Seymour Lipsett, "The Egghead Looks at Himself," *New York Times Magazine* November 17, 1957, p. 22ff.

25. Tugwell, *The Democratic Roosevelt*, pp. 9, 218ff., 326ff. William M. McGovern and David Collier, *Radicals and Conservatives*, Chicago, Regnery 1958, relate the traditional "Burkean" position to liberal epistemology on a basis of scientism, according to Stanley Parry's review in National Review, April 12, 1958, p. 354.

26. "Revolution," *U.S.A.*, August 10, 1956, pp. 349-354. Cf. William A. Rusher in National Review, March 22, 1958, p. 283, "Only since the growth of the deadly notion that a man's mind is a tribunal superior to any law derived from governments or God, have large numbers of men joined hands to betray, in conscious stealth, the lands of their birth."

27. A review of Alan Bullock and Maurice Shock, *The Liberal Tradition from Fox to Keynes*, TLS, November 23, 1956.

28. Dresser quotes from Malcolm McDermott, in *Spotlight for the Nation*, No. F373-4, Febuary 2, 1957. On the dangers of weakening local government, see *Closer-Up—Don Bell Reports*, February 21, 1958, "The Story of 1313."

29. *Dan Smoot Report*, December 9, 1957.

30. Frank Chodorov, *The Income Tax, Root of All Evil*, New York, Devin-Adair, 1954 *Dawn*, published by Sherwood C. Ide's Independence Foundation, is the official organ of Orfit (the Organization to Repeal the Federal Income Tax).

31. Stone's testimony before the House Ways and Means Committe in support of a proposed constitutional amendment to repeal the income tax was read into the *Congressional Record* of February 18, 1958, by Ralph Gwinn.

32. See Robert E. Dresser, *Spotlight for the Nation, loc. cit.* and *Congressional Record*, March 6, 1958 for an article by David Lawrence read into the *Record* by Representative Sadlak.

33. Edward A. Rumely, *Memorandum*, March 11, 1958; George Racey Jordan, *Gold and Freedom*, Committee for a Free Gold Market, 1957; Howard E. Kershner, *God, Gold and Government*, Englewood, New Jersey, Prentice-Hall, 1957; William Ropke, *The Economics of Full Employment*, 1952, pp. 22-25. See also Herbert C. Holdridge, "Petition against the Federal Reserve Bank," March 25, 1958, and Eustance Mullins, *The Federal Reserve Conspiracy*, Union, New Jersey, Common Sense Press, 1954, and compare *Monetary Notes*, journal of the Economists' National Committee on Monetary Policy, April 1, 1958.

34. *From Major Jordan's Diaries*, New York, Harcourt Brace, 1952. The quotations are from Lester O. Wisler, *Economic Liberty*, Oakland, California, Liberty Free Press, 1958. Cf. *The Cross and the Flag, March* 1958, p. 6, and April 1958, p. 30

35. Monroe W. Karmin, "Social Security, Benefit or Burden?" *American Mercury*, March 1958, p. 113. See also Dillard Stokes, *Social Security: Fact and Fancy*, Chicago, Regnery, 1956; Lewis A. Aleson, *The Physician's Responsibility as Leader*, Caldwell, Caxton, 1953; *IUD Digest*, Spring, 1958, p. 58.

36. See David Shea Teeple, "Are Subsidies Sinful Only for Socialists?" *Human Events*, December 21, 1957 "Subsidies are doubly sinful for capitalists. First, because it is inconsistent for them to oppose a 'handout' for others but to accept one themselves; and second, because subsidies lead to the regimentation of the economy under

state socialism." Cf. Arthur Kemp, *The Role of Government in Developing Peaceful Uses of Atomic Energy*, American Enterprise Association pamphlet, 1956, p. 47: "The sooner a maximum degree of freedom can be given to industry, including the freedom to lose money, the more likely we are to discover the most economical forms of reactors and the less likely we are to misuse our resources." See also Price Daniel, "Federal versus States' Rights in the Tidelands Cases," *Spotlight for the Nation* No. B-125, and the Committee for Contitutional Government's statement, "The Octopus on the Potomas." And compare Verne Kaub's *Follies, Fallacies, and Falsehoods of Tennessee Valley Authority* issued by the American Council of Christian Laymen.

37. "New Dealers—Then and Now," *Human Events*, December 14, 1957.

38. Philip D. Bradley, Involuntary Participation in Unionism, AEA pamphlet, 1956. See also the newsletters of the National Right to Work Committee; *Exclusive*, January-April 1958; *Human Events*, December 28, 1957, "The Coming Labor Struggle": "Such a reform [outlawing the closed shop] would—it is obvious—cut down drastically the whole political, economic and social structure of the New and Fair Deals." See also the intercollegiate debate materials distributed by the National Association of Manufacturers, which includes *A Monograph Discussing the Major Aspects of the Intercollegiate Debate Issue;* Edward Maher, *The Hot Fight over the Right to Work;* Leo Wolman, *Labor Monopoly and Its Implications to a Free Society;* Karl Mundt, *What's Ahead in the Senate Labor Investigations?* and *The United States Is Only 37½ per cent Free!*—a map indicating those states "which ban forced unionism." Also the U.S. Chamber of Commerce urged the McCellan Committee to ignore "corruption" in unions and instead to take up "the secondary boycott, compulsory unionism (the union shop), application of anti-trust laws to unions and abuse of picketing as it affects the public." (*Washington Window*, April 4, 1958). These arguments would all come more gracefully from those who had less to gain by them.

39. *Closer Up*, March 7, 1958; *The Economic Facts of Life*, X, 2, February 1957, to be used "in employee magazines, in executive communications and as sermons and classroom material;" Hoffer, *The True Believer*, p. 133,; Tugwell, *The Democratic Roosevelt*, pp. 251-252; Herbert Hoover, *American Ideals versus the New Deal*, New York, Scribner Press, [n. d.].

40. This idea was always an essential part of puritanism, as Tawney pointed out long ago, quoting, for example, R. Young, *The Poore's Advocate*, 1654, p. 6: "No question but that riches should be the portion rather of the godly than of the wicked . . . for godliness hath the promises of this life as well as of the life to come." (R. H. Tawney, *Religion and the Rise of Captalsm*, New York, Harcourt Brace, 1926, p. 267). And it was closely tied to the doctrine of individualism in America, especially, where the the gospel of work has been deeply intrenched. It is still a favorite right wing doctrine, and appears often in Howard Kershner's *Christian Economics*. See also Ray Carroll, *Jesus a Capitalist*, published by the American Council of Christian Laymen, 1952, p. 11: "Jesus worked with his father in the construction business . . . Necessarily, Joseph and Son were small contractors, and as sober and skillful men, prospered as such . . . There was no labor union to meddle with prices and wages. Prices were fixed in the natural way, by haggling . . . The father and son fixed their prices in competition, low bidder to win . . . Read about the talents, and the workers in the vineyard; business was business in Nazareth, as it is here today . . . Jesus was a capitalist, preaching a doctrine of individualism which is the basis of free enterprise." And cf. Alfred P. Haake, *Faith and Fact. A Guide to Economics through Christian*

Understanding, Harrisburg, Pennsylvania, Stackpole, 1953, and Edward A. Keller, *Christianity and American Capitalism*, Chicago, Heritage, 1953.

41. *U.S.A.*, February 1, 1957. See also *Which Council?* a pamphlet released by the American Council of Christian Churches c1945, pp. 5-6: "Social evils may be eradicated only...when men, one by one (even as men are born) are born again as new creatures in Jesus Christ."

42. *Portions in Due Season*, March 1958, p. 10; *Herald of His Coming*, March 1958; Edgar C. Bundy, *Collectivism in the Churches*, Wheaton, Illinois, Church League of America, 1958, p. ix.

43. Spring, 1958.

44. March, 1958.

45. See the affidavit signed by ex-communist Kenneth Goff, director of Soldiers of the Cross, on Communist use of fluorides, Report of the UN-American Activities Committee, vol. 9, 1939. Reprinted in *The Malist*, August 1957: "We discussed quite thoroughly the fluoridation of water supplies and how we were using it in Russia as a tranquilizer in the prison camps. The leaders of our school felt that if it could be induced into the American water supply, it would bring about a spirit of lethargy in the nation; where it would keep the general public docile during a steady encroachment of communism. We also discussed the fact that keeping a store of deadly fluorine near the water reservoir would be advantageous during the time of the revolution as it would give us opportunity to dump this poison into the water supply and either kill off the population or threaten them with liquidation, so they would surrender to obtain fresh water." This appears to be an earlier source than Major Jordan's account, but Jordan was quoted for sometime before Goff. Many new groups have been organized especially to fight fluoridation, and there is a Citizens' Committee against Flouridation or a Pure Water Association in almost every state, with county and city branches. *The National Fluoridation News* is the chief organ of these groups, though there are many other papers besides. Many writers give as their source for the communist plot, the works of George Racey Jordan, especially *From Major Jordan's Diaries, op. cit.*, p. 170, and *Fluoridation of Water*, Ridgefield, Connecticut, Coalition Enterprises, 1956.

The list of symptoms mentioned here is found in *National Fluoridation News*, June 1956, p. 4. See also the publications of the following groups, 1955-58; American Flag Committee, esp. *Newsletter* No. 40; American Public Relations Forum, *Bulletin* No. 71, April 1958; Borger, Texas, *News-Herald;* California Minute Women of the USA; Congress of Freedom's *Freedom Facts;* Council of Public Affairs; *New Mexico Women Speak; Women's Voice*. It might surprise these people to learn that the *Daily Worker*, in a review of F. B. Exner and G. L. Waldbott, *The American Fluoridation Experiment*, ed. James Rorty, New York, Devin-Adair, 1957, came out also against fluoridation. This book is one of the scriptures of the right wing and deserves a wider audience. See also *Look*, June 24, 1958, for a general article favoring fluoridation, which *Right* accuses of misrepresentation (August 1958).

The claim, frequently appearing in the *National Fluoridation News*, that the aluminum trusts and chemical companies are behind this plot in order to make a fast buck out of a waste product, seems more suitable for leftists, but is usually employed by rightists. In the same way the right has recently taken up the old leftist cry against life insurance rates; and *Human Events* and *I. F. Stone's Weekly* reacted identically to the Rockefeller Report.

46. See Emanuel M. Josephson, *Rockefeller, Internationalist*, New York, Chedney,

1952; Morris A. Bealle's *American Capsule News;* Upton Close' *Closer Up* (now edited by George Deatherage and Don Bell); Gerald Winrod's *The Defender* (now edited by William T. Watson); Leon DeAryan's *The Broom* (also called *The Aryan Sun Workshop*); and William Kullgren's *The Beacon Light Herald.* Cf. the press releases of J. Richard Feeley, Louis Pauly, the Massachusetts Women's Political Society, and the Boston Nutrition Society. For cosmetics see especially, A. Lovell's *Kingdom Digest.* The Reward Beauty System is "a unique enterprise in which the highest grade of cosmetics is dedicated to the promotion of the greatest message, 'Jesus preaching the Kingdom of God," Kenneth Goff, author of *Brainwashing, Reds Promote Racial War,* the fluoridation affidavit quoted above, and other favorite right wing tracts, is on the Board of Directors. For Reich's accumulator see *Voice of Creation,* January 1958.

47. *Free Men Speak,* February 15, 1955. Now called *The Independent American.*

48. *Bible News Flashes,* March 1958.

49. *Grass Roots,* August 1955, p. 9.

50. *Congressional Record,* May 7, 1956, p. 6728ff. An excellent survey of the literature on this position is found in the newsletters of the Shearon Legislative Service. See also the files of *The Green Mountain Rifleman.* Note that Priscella Buckley opposes the right wing stand on mental health. See *Bulletin* of the American Public Relations Forum.

51. On Kasper's testimony, see *Look,* February 19, 1957, p. 30. Anthony J. Marino in *The World Conspiracy* (Chicago, 1957) goes even further than Kasper. "Psychiatry," he says, "is treason." It sometimes seems that the Right distrusts Freud even more than Marx, so that it appears unlikely that the third world war will be fought, as Peter Nathan supposes (*Retreat From Reason,* London, Heineman, 1955, p. 211) between the Freudians and the Marxists. For the ACLU statements, see *Civil Liberties,* March 1958, and *Nor Speak with Double Tongue,* ACLU pamphlet, June 1957, p. 71; pp. 80-81. (Note also p. 70 that ACLU is helping Gerald L. K. Smith in his effort to get his party on the state ballot.) See also Jack LaZebnik, "The Case of Ezra Pound," *New Republic,* April 1, 1957, pp. 17-20, and Richard Rovere, "The Question of Ezra Pound," *Esquire,* September 1957, p. 66ff. and February 1958, p. 22B. The Pound case, of course, is now happily resolved.

52. *Analysis of the Ray Murphy Committee Report on UNESCO,* by the Americanism Commission of the American Legion, 8th District, Department of Texas, Houston, 1955, p. 5.

53. *U.S.A.,* February 28, 1958, p. 4.

54. *U.S.A., loc. cit.,* p. 5.

55. Cedar Rapids, Iowa, *Gazette,* March 30, 1958, p. 1. One of the most disturbing things to many writers about the Alaska hospital was the great quality of land ceded to its use. This actually amounted to a land grant, and, as in the case of the land grant colleges, the income from the lands is to be used for maintenance. Most right wingers saw this enormous tract of land as a site for an infinite number of prison camps, since no ordinary hospital would require such extensive grounds.

Occasionally rightists have reversed this identification of insanity with conservatism. See E. L. Anderson in *Right* No. 20: "Only a sick mind (a liberal mind) would choose to go down without fighting." And one reads with some astonishment the remarks before the Un-American Activities Committee, on May 29, 1957, of Frederick Charles Schwarz, "one of the few whom the Committee asked to testify," according to *Dan Smoot's Report:* "I believe that paranoia is at the heart of communism." Not only that, but to suppose that we can negotiate with the Soviets shows "a failure to understand communism so completely that it approaches mental illness." (April 7, 1958, pp. 5-6) Dr. Schwarz is Director of the Christian Anti-Communist Crusade. Perhaps this is the beginning of a new trend.

56. Golden Report, 1956. It is worth noting that the Legion, while fighting most social legislation for the general public, has actually been a liberalizing influence in promoting it *for veterans*. If the GI Bill had not proved to be such an excellent thing for education in America, there might be less talk of federal aid for education now.

On the unclaimed scholarships, see the *Wall Street Journal*, March 1958; Mort Weisinger in *Better Homes and Gardens*, June 1957; *Human Events*, March 17, 1958. See also Ralph W. Gwinn, "Federal Scholarships—What For?" *National Republic*, April 1958, p. 1ff, and *Congressional Record*, January 15, 1958. On luxurious buildings, see the *Bulletins* of the Council for Basic Education and Dorothy Thompson, "Do American Educators Know What They Are Up To?" *Ladies Home Journal*, February, 1958. An excellent survey of the whole right wing position appears in Frances Bartlett's *Facts in Education*, March-April, 1958.

57. McDonald's suorce for Russian history is Demetri Demiaskevitch, *Activity Program in Russia*. A more detailed study of this same material appears in Augustin Rudd's *Bending the Twig: The Revolution in Education and Its Effect on Our Children*, Chicago, Heritage, 1957, a book which was widely distributed by right wing organizations and summarized in the *American Mercury*, January 1958. Representative Ralph Gwinn read this summary into the *Congressional Record* on January 27, 1958. *American Magazine*, October 1954. See especially the other publications of the American Education Association, Defenders of American Education, Guardians of American Education, and see *Facts in Education* and the *Educational Reviewer*. See also Mary L. Allen, *Education or Indoctrination*, Caldwell, Idaho, Caxton, 1955; William F. Buckley, *God and Man at Yale*, Chicago, Regnery, 1951; Bella V. Dodd, *School of Darkness*, New York, P. J. Kennedy, 1954; Kitty Jones and Robert Olivier, *Progressive Education Is Reeducation*, Boston, Meador, 1956, Verne Kaub, *Communist-Socialist Propaganda in American Schools*, Boston, Meador, 1953, and *Satan Goes to School*, American Council pamphlet, 1952; Freda Koch, *Federal Aid: Trap for the Unwary*, American Council pamphlet, 1957; E. Merrill Root, *Collectivism on the Campus*, New York, Devin-Adair, 1955; Paul W. Shafer and John Howland Snow, *The Turning of the Tides*, New York, Long House, 1953; Mortimer Smith, *And Madly Teach, The Diminished Mind*, and *The Public Schools in Crisis*, Chicago, Regnery, 1950, 1954, 1956.   h

See also Alice Widener's "Letter to My Daughter," *U.S.A.*, December 20, 1957, in which the awarding of gold stars for merit, and the wearing of dresses by girls appear as symbols of the superior education in Catholic, as opposed to "progressive" schools. See also her "Letter for My Grandchild," *U.S.A.*, August 2, 1957. Mrs. Widener received a Freedoms Foundation award for this second letter, joining the company of Herbert Hoover and J. Edgar Hoover, earlier recipients.

58. *America First Actimust Bulletin*, May, 1954. *Dan Smoot Report*, December 9, 1957, p. 4. See also J. Edgar Hoover, "God and Country or Communism," *American Legion Magazine*, November 1957: "Scores of indivduals who have never been members of the communist organization contribute to the spread of the philosophy of materialism. In so doing they are adding generously to the strength of the communist movement. Among these philosophic materialists are numerous educators, authors and lecturers." Hoover is quoted by W. Hume Everett in *News and Views*, April 1958, p. 1: "The pseudo-liberal can be more destructive than the communist because

of the esteem which his cloak of respectability invites." See also Roger C. Dunn, *The Political 'H' Bomb*, Dunn Survey, 1958, who states that liberalism is the back door of socialism which is the back door of communism; *Facts in Education*, May-June, 1957: "the public schools have, within our time, become battlegrounds in the struggle between 'conservative' Americans and the new alien-type cult called 'liberals' "; Pete White in *Christian Crusade Magazine*, May 1957, p. 4: "We must ... pay tribute to the man who has led this mighty Crusade against the forces of Communism, apostacy and liberalism." See also the literature distributed by the Harvard Veritas Society in opposition to J. Robert Oppenheimer and Arthur Schlesinger, Jr., and by the Friends of the Aquinas Foundation at Princeton, in support of Father Halton's charges of atheism and communism at Princeton.

On the question of school curricula, General Mark Clark's remarks to Citadel alumni have been much quoted: "No conception of the doctrine of academic freedom should or could ever extend to give a group of teachers the right to ignore the wishes of the people who pay the bills, who are the owners and who run the schools." The situation is similar, he explains, "to freedom of the press." (*Augusta Courier*, November 12, 1956.)

59. See Frank Chodorov, "Civil Rights versus Natural Rights," *Human Events*, March 30, 1957; Noah M. Mason, "Civil Rights' against the Constitution," *Human Events*, July 13, 1957. See also other issues of *Human Events* and of *Exclusive*, 1957 and 1958, for comment on Nixon and Knowland, and compare *The Cross and the Flag, Over Here, Free Men Speak, Right*, and the *Bulletin* of the California Constitution Party for September 1957. Arguments against the right wing position are marshalled by Sidney Hook, "Democracy and Desegregation," *New Leader*, Section 2, April 14, 1958.

60. See Robert M. MacIver, *Academic Freedom in Our Time*, New York, Columbia, 1955; Henry Steele Commager, "Why Are We Mad at Teacher?" *Reporter*, October 21, 1954, pp. 39-40; Malcolm Cowley, "Who Are the Intellectuals?" *New Republic*, February 25, 1957; "More Power to the Nightstick," *Human Events*, October 26, 1957; Ernest Van Den Haag, "Communism, Democracy and Religion," *National Review*, March 22, 1958, pp. 275 77; *Faith and Freedom*, April 1956.

61. John K. Crippen, "Facts and Fancies," Des Plaines, Illinois, *Surburban Times*, March 6, 1958.

62. Often quoted is the passage in Don Whitehead's *The FBI Story*, New York, Random House, 1956, in which Hoover puts aside the crown of power. One of the few dissenting opinions arrives unsigned from Miami, Florida, April 5, 1958, pointing out that Hoover, in his new book, *Masters of Deceit*, credits the B'nai B'rith with effective opposition to communism, and asks, "Is he so badly compromised as to be forced to become a part of the conspiracy?" Other Hoover admirers will find very disturbing his valiant effort in this book to seperate the communist conspiracy from American Jewish organizations, Zionism, and the NAACP. See especially *Closer Up*, April 4, 1958, where it is claimed that "The Synagogue of Satan has 'captured' the last great citadel of officialdom, the office of the director of the Federal Bureau of Investigation." *I. F. Stone's Weekly* (May 12, 1958), on the other hand, feels that Hoover says "nothing which could offend any white supremacist." See also Fred J. Cook, "The F.B.I.," *The Nation*, Special Issue, October 18, 1958.

63. *Bulletin* of the Federation for Constitutional Government, March 1958, quoting from Eastland's speech to the National Society of New England Women, January 23, 1958. See also *Exclusive*, March 26, 1958; and William E. Jenner, "What Is the

Supreme Court's Appellate Jurisdiction?" *American Mercury*, March 1958, pp. 26-27. The punitive attitude toward the court appears further in Frederick Nelson's hope: "Maybe Bill Jenner . . . has scared 'em a little." Chicago *Daily News*, April 28, 1958.

64. James O. Eastland, "An Alien's Ideology Is Not the Law of Our Republic," *American Mercury*, March 1958, pp. 28-29. Cf. John Crippen, *loc. cit.*, "The Supreme Court . . . has in effect re-written the U. S. Constitution, has based its decisions upon whimsy, 'social scientist' crackpots, such as Gunnar Myrdal, and upon a complete reversal, in many cases, of legal and constitutional precepts." Cf. R. Carter Pittman, "The Law of the Land," *Journal of Public Law*, Emory University Law School, Georgia, 1958.

65. Rosalie M. Gordon, *Nine Men against America*, New Rochelle, New York, America's Future, Inc., p. 14. Cf. Verne Kaub in *The Virginian*, February 1956, p. 3, similarly pointing out that this decision must be fought as a states' rights issue, and not in racial terms, though the *Virginian*, in general, has not accepted this advice, nor has Kaub's *Challenge*, March 1958.

66. See P. D. East, "Claudy's Column," *The Petal Paper*, May 9, 1957, p. 4, for a satirical treatment of this theme. There are certainly some right wing organizations that favor integration, but none has come to light in the present survey. One occasionally reads that integration was proceeding very successfully before the Supreme Court interferred, suggesting that the writer considers integration ultimately desirable, in some other age.

67. Gordon, p. 19; p. 22.

68. *New Republic*, August 26, 1957; *Free Men Speak*, August 1957, p. 2.

69. *The Cross and the Flag*, October 1957, p. 12. American Bar Association *Journal*, January 1958, p. 35ff. Cf. Warren Jefferson Davis' review of James J. Kilpatrick, *The Sovereign States* (Chicago, Regnery, 1957) in the *Journal*, February 1958, p. 159ff, in which the reviewer quotes Senator Stennis: a "continuing series of mongrel, psychological rulings . . . based not upon law, but upon hyper-theoretical phantasy." These articles are partially balanced by that of Thomas C. Hennings in the March 1958 issue, though here one also finds W. H. Rehnquist protesting the bar admission cases. The Bar Association officially opposed the Jenner bill, however. On the question of limiting civil liberties to secure national survival, see also the recent study by Walter Burns, *Freedom, Virtue and the First Amendment*, Baton Rouge, Louisiana, State University Press, 1957. See also Robert Morris' speech to the New York State Convention of the American Legion, "Time is Running Out," reprinted in *Common Sense*, March 15, 1958; *The Councilor Newsletter's* remarks about Learned Hand's book *The Bill of Rights*, Cambridge, Harvard, 1958; the address of Ernest G. Swigert, President of the National Association of Manufacturers, before the Congress of American Industry, read into the *Congressional Record* by Ralph Gwinn, January 27, 1958; Herman E. Talmadge, *You and Segregation*, Birmingham, Vulcan, 1955; and R. Carter Pittman, "The Supreme Court, the Broken Constitution and the Shattered Bill of Rights," reprinted in Talmadge's *The Statesman*, January 1956.

70. The *locus classicus* for this sentiment is of course George Washington's Farewell Address, quoted from time to time in every right wing paper.

71. Cf. the various sociological explanations given for this problem in Bell, *The New American Right*. Observe, incidentally, that many right wing names listed in this paper are obviously not Anglo-Saxon names.

72. The talk of hyphenated Americans goes back a long way. William Roscoe Thayer, *Democracy: Discipline: Peace* (Boston, 1919) spoke of recent immigrants

as "mongrels with a divided allegiance ... hypenates, whose hyphen, like the kiss of Judas, is a link for treachery." Even Theodore Roosevelt, in a message dictated the night before he died to the American Defense Society, declared: "There can be no divided allegiance here. Any man who says he is an American, but something else also, isn't an American at all. We have room for but one flag, and this excludes the red flag, which symbolizes all wars against liberty and civilization ... We have room for but one language here, and that is the English language, for we intend to see that the crucible turns our people out as Americans, of American nationality, and not as dwellers in a polyglot boarding house; and we have room for but one soul loyalty, and that is loyalty to the American people." *American Defense*, October 1943, p. 2. It is characteristic of those who speak of hyphenates to assume that it is the new, and not the older, Americans who supply the hyphen; whereas the record suggests that our immigrants have always been desperately eager to acquire 100 per cent Americanism.

73. "The War against our Immigration Law," *Human Events*, April 20, 1957, and "The Truth about the Immigration Act," *Reader's Digest*, May 1953. Anderson, Chairman of the Commission's Sub committee on Immigration and Naturalization, gave this testimony before the Senate Judicary Subcommittee. The Resolutions of the Coalition, adopted on February 16,1956, are reported in the Borger, Texas, *News-Herald*, May 11, 1956. The Coalition also distributes reprints of J. B. Matthews, "Immigration, 1956 Issue," *American Mercury*, October 1955. See also Archibald Roosevelt, *Conquest via Immigration*, New York, The Alliance, 1956.

74. Richard Arens, *Our Immigration System—A First Line of Defense*, Address to the National Society on April 18, 1957. See also the DAR Resolutions, April 14-18, 1952; and cf. the Resolutions of the Iowa chapter for 1958. Colonel Bluford H. J. Balter writes in the *Small Business Review*, June 1951, p. 15. See the Platform of the American Action Council, Inc. The Realpolitical Institute, Letter of January 1, 1957.

The old myth of Nordic supremacy still finds considerable support from the right; and is sometimes curiously justified by those who accept the Anglo-Israel message— the notion that the Anglo-Saxon-Scandinavian (and sometimes Celtic) peoples have literally descended from Abraham through Issac and the lost ten tribes, and that Jews are descended from the tribe of Judah only. In current American publications this belief seems largely to reinforce anti-Jewish tendencies (though such writers as John Monk do not accept it), but some years earlier it created great enthusiasm for Zionism among the British. William B. Ziff, *The Rape of Palestine* (reprinted in *Middle East and the West I*, 3) explains Zionism as the creation of the Anglo-Israelite Association. See also Edmund Wilson's essay, "The Jews," in his recent collection, *A Piece of My Mind*, New York, Farrar, 1956.

75. Victor Milione, editor of the Intercollegiate Society of Individualists' *Individualist*, denies a double standard here, declaring that he militantly defends the Rightist's rights because they are in the greatest present danger. "We are part of the 'all' mentioned in the Declaration of Independence." Milione is on the somewhat safer ground here of the 'rights' of American Communists rather than of American Negroes, but presumably he would extend his ideas of coercion to this area also. It is difficult to present this argument in an enlightened way, and Milione needs help.

76. The incongruous identification of abstract art, dissonant or jazz music, and stream-of-consciousness writing with communism is peculiarly American Right Wing, just as identifying it with decadent capitalism is peculiarly Communist. Both sides are just beginning to be able to take a little Joyce. See *American Legion Magazine*, April 1958, pp. 6-7, for the usual Philistine approach. The great critic of modern art

in Congress has of course been Representative George A. Dondero. See the *Congressional Record*, June 14, 1956. See also *American Legion Firing Line*, February 1, and 15, 1955, and September 1, 1956; *Counterattack*, April 4, 1958. These later articles discuss not the art but the artist and his "citations." American jazz and "rock and roll" has come in for some bitter excoriation because of its Negro origin and supposed licentious nature. *The Virginian*, November 1956, sees jazz as seducing youth and corrupting race; January 1957: Schools which encourage rock and roll are encouraging "the vilest possible aspect of carnal nature." See also the reports of Mrs. Anne Smart and the Indiana PTA Study Group on pornography in school libraries.

This is not to say, of course, that there are not Rightists with sound literary and artistic values. One finds much to admire in recent book reviews, for example, in the *National Review*, particularly William Buckley on James Gould Cozzens at Whittaker Chambers on Ayn Rand. The general support of Ezra Pound is to be commended from any point of view.

77. Styles Bridges, "Keep the Experts on 'Tap' but Not on 'Top'," *loc. cit.* See also the Oppenheimer controversy in the letters of the Harvard Veritas Society.

78. *The Truth about the United Nations; the Speeches, Findings and Resolutions of the Congress of Freedom,Inc.*, San Francisco, 1955. On Nathan Hale, see *The Educational Signpost*, March 1956, p. 3. Dr. Lindsey, minister of the First Presbyterian Church, Tacoma, Washington, is quoted in *National Republic*, March 1958, p. 12. On bi-partisan acceptance of the UN, see Bradford Westerfield, *Foreign Policy and Party Politics, Pearl Harbor to Korea*, New Haven, Yale Press, 1955.

79. American Council of Christian Churches, Letters to Congress; Balter, in *Small Business Review*, *loc. cit.* A report from the late Col. Balter (New Orleans *Item*, February 4, 1958) finds him still disturbed by "the Communistic Manifesto and confiscatory taxes," and recommending that we "abolish his (Mr. Dulles') position and clean out the State Department clean," but nonetheless rejoicing in the added commerce that will come to the Mississippi River from the St. Lawrence Seaway. Quite a sea-change.

80. Matthews, *Christian Crusade Magazine*, February 1958. See the platform of the Abraham Lincoln Republican Club, the annual resolutions of the DAR, SAR, American Legion, American Coalition of Patriotic Societies, Congress of Freedom, Convention of We the People, and the Citizens Foreign Relations Committee. See the Freedom Club Questionnaire, the *Dan Smoot Reports*, the platform of the Constitution Party, U.S.A., the opinions of Herbert Philbrick in *U.S.A.* December 7, 1956, and the program of the American Heritage Protective Committee.

81. *Human Events*, March 10, 1958; Braden's address was given to the American Coalition of Patriotic Societies and read into the *Congressional Record* by Ralph Gwinn, February 6, 1958. Reprints were distributed by the *Christian Journal*. See Braden's additional comments, *Manion Forum*, March 16, 1958, and cf. Thurman Sensing, *The Case against Foreign Aid*, distributed with the *Bulletin* of the Southern States Industrial Council, March 1, 1958. See also the books of Eugene W. Castle, *Billions, Blunders and Baloney*, New York, Devin-Adair, 1955, and *The Great Giveaway*, Chicago, Regnery, 1957, and see the account of his Congressional testimony in the Chicago *Tribune*, March 28, 1958, p. 3.

82. *Right*, May 1956, p. 1, makes the customary identification of the right wing with anti-communism. But such anti-communist groups as the Council against Communist Aggression and the American-Asian Educational Exchange are made up of both liberal and conservative members.

83. For one detailed account of the classical conspiracy, see William Guy Carr, "The Conspiracy to Destroy All Existing Governments and Religions," *News behind the News*, National Federation of Christian Laymen, April 1958. Other frequently cited sources include the works of Eric D. Butler, Cherep-Spiridovich, Herbert Sanborn, E. N. Sanctuary, John Creagh Scott, Nesta H. Webster, Robert H. Williams. For some account of earlier uses of this material, see Eric F. Goldman, *The Crucial Decade*, Chapter VI, and Richard Hofstadter, *The Age of Reform*, New York, Knopf, 1955. See also "The Brotherhood," *American Mercury*, March 1958. Archibald Roosevelt, *Manual for American Action*, New York, The Alliance, [n. d.] p. 16; Dangerous to the Right are those who "are convinced that some group of men, or some religious sect, or some race, has been carrying on a secret conspiracy for thousands of years."

For some comment on "conspiracy" charges against labor, see Fred and Marie Haug, *A New Attack on Labor and Civil Liberties*, Cleveland, Ohio, 1958. The left has suffered from belief in various conspiracy theories, too, such as the "corporate monopoly" conspiracy described by Brandeis, Wilson and LaFollette and popularized by Roosevelt; the international munitions-maker's conspiracy reported by Archibald MacLeish; and mo re recently the notion of conspiracy among the Madison Avenue brainwashers. See Vance Packard's *The Hidden Persuaders*, New York, McKay, 1957, and M. S. Evans' review in *Human Events*, September 14, 1957.

84. *Closer Up*, March 7, 1958.

85. The cesspool figure recurs frequently in all conspiracy literature along with various other images of filth and ordure. Robert Powell Leroy, the "Paratrooper Preacher," quotes characteristically from Joseph McCarthy: "The educational system of this Country cannot be cleansed of Communist influence by legislation. It can only be scrubbed and flushed and swept clean if the mothers and fathers, and the sons and daughters, of this nation individually decide to do this job." (*The Alarming Cry* II, 2 p. 4) So also Paul Harvey, rightist radio commentator, speaking to the Conservative Citizens Committee in Minneapolis, said, "I didn't like Joe McCarthy's methods and Joe didn't like them either. If there had been some nice genteel way to clean up a mess that no decent farmer would be willing to track into his house, Joe would have used it." (Iowa Civil Liberties Union *Bulletin*, February 1, 1958, p. 4)

86. *The Revere*, March 1958, 1. 3. Adams is editor of *Integration News*, published by the Southern States Press Association in Washington.

87. *New Leader*, April 7, 1958, p. 11. Russell and Hook have been debating this question in recent issues of the *New Leader*.

88. *Loc. cit.*, II, 2. p. 3.

89. Letter of November 29, 1956.

90. *The Cross and the Flag*, December 1957, p. 2.

91. *American Mercury*, November 1956, and June 1956. See Notes 78 and 80. Eph. 6:12 is frequently quoted, as by the *Georgia Tribune* (April 10, 1958): "for we wrestle not against flesh and blood, but against principalities, against powers, against the rulers of the darkness of this world; against Spiritual wickedness in high places."

92. "The Quality of the South," *National Review*, March 8, 1958, pp. 236-237.

93. *Right*, May 1956, p. 1, See also n. 58.

94. *The Southern Conservative*, February 1958, p. 6. J. Edgar Hoover, "The American Ideal," Address at Freedoms Foundation Annual Awards, February 22, 1957, and *American Legion Magazine*, November 1957. For a summary of the historical use of the terms *liberal* and *progressive*, see Eric Goldman, *Rendevous with Destiny*,

New York, Knopf, 1952. For accounts of the treachery of New Deal, Fair Deal, and Big Deal government see *Human Events*, May 11, 1957; Bryton Barron, *Inside the State Department*, New York, 1957; Morris A. Bealle, *Washington Squirrel Cage*, Washington, Columbia, 1952; Elizabeth Churchill Brown, *The Enemy at His Back*, New York, Bookmailer, 1956;: James Burnham, *The Web of Subversion*, New York, Day 1954; Larston D. Farrar, *Washington Lowdown*, New York, Signet, 1956; John T. Flynn, *The Decline of the American Republic*, New York, Devin-Adair, 1955; Joseph Kamp, *Trickery, Treachery, Tyranny and Treason in Washington*, New York, Headlines, 1957; Robert Littleton, *An Era of Infamy*, Cleveland, 1952; Douglas MacArthur, *Revitalizing a Nation*, Chicago, Heritage, 1952; Chesly Manly, *The Twenty-Year Revolution*, Chicago Regnery, 1954; Felix Wittmer, *The Conquest of the American Mind*, Boston, Meador, 1950; Harry Elmer Barnes, *Perpetual War for Perpetual Peace*, Caldwell, Idaho, Caxton, 1953; Garet Garrett *The Peoples Pottage and The American Story*, Caldwell, Caxton, 1953 and 1954.

For a more recent comment, see the *Dan Smoot Report*, April 14, 1958: "Practically all influential 'liberals' in America, although regarding themselves as anticommunist, want the same kind of society that communists are after; they want a total transfer of political power from the individual to government, so that government can regulate the level and redistribute wealth...American 'liberals' will not accept the evidence that socialism must inevitably end in total disaster...Thus under 'liberal' leadership, our national effort to resist the spread of communism is aimless and confused and self-contradictory."

95. Courtney Whitney: *MacArthur: His Rendevous with History*, New York, Knopf, 1956. Cf. Charles A. Willoughby's *Shanghai Conspiracy*, New York, Dutton, 1952.

96. *Battle Line I, 2*, January 22, 1958. *The Seeds of Treason*, New York, *Newsweek*, 1950. A biography of Richard Nixon by DeToledano was published in 1956.

97. *National Review*, May 25, 1957, p. 496ff. Cf. Medford Evans' ingenious explanation of Oppenheimer's distaste for making the H bomb: his knowledge that he must turn over the recipe to his Kremlin masters (*National Review*, March 9, 1957).

98. *Ibid*, March 22, 1958, p. 283. Rusher is reviewing Morris's recent book, *No Wonder We Are Losing*, New York, Bookmailer, 1958. See also Robert E. Stripling, *The Red Plot against America*, ed. Bob Considine, Drexel Hill, Bell, 1949; and see Will Watson, "Conservative Patriots Can Organize," *American Mercury*, March 1958, pp. 124-127.

99. Sidney Hook, in reviewing John Cogley's *Report on Blacklisting* (New York, Fund for the Republic, 1956) in the New York *Times*, July 22, 1956, p. 6, suggests that a flaw in Cogley's discussion is his failure to distinguish between admitted Communists who do work for the dictatorship of the proletariat and those who have been falsely charged with Communist activities. Cogley, according to Hook, deplores the witch-hunting of the latter, but doesn't quite say that a true Communist shouldn't be blacklisted either. Apparently this is a point on which many lefists had not quite made up their minds until the Supreme Court did it for them.

100. A typical list is given in *Behind the Communist Line*, February-March, 1958, pp. 3-4. Another was issued by the State Department. *Notes: Soviet Affairs* No. 216, November 6, 1957. Senator Styles Bridges declared that the Soviets have kept only three of forty agreements made (*Human Events*, May 12, 1958).

101. John Kennedy, "A Democrat Looks at Foreign Policy," *Foreign Affairs*, October 1957, p. 46: "At times in recent years it has been hard to distinguish Secretary Dulles'

emphatic reaffirmation of the imminent collapse of Soviet totalitarianism from the wooden Marxist-Stalinist view of the essential fragility of the capitalist order." In the same issue of *Foreign Affairs*, however, Dulles' "Challenge and Response in U.S. Policy," speaks less of imminent collapse than of "the yeast of change" which will work imperceptibly, and will require time (p. 28.). But see also Alfred Kohlberg in an open letter to Bertrand Russell, April 9, 1958, on the program of his Citizens' Foreign Relations Committee: "With Secretary Dulles, they believe that a regime that dares not risk a free election after 40 years of monopolized control of press, radio, education, all organizations, and of election machinery, can be no more than a 'passing phase.'" *Human Events* (May 12, 1958) quotes John Noble, *I Was a Slave in Russia*, New York, Devin-Adair, 1958; "There will soon be uprisings, not only in the prison camps, but all over Russia."

102. See Donald W. Treadgold, "Forty Years of Communism," *New Republic*, September 30, 1957, pp. 18-19, and Lucille Cardin Crain in *Free Enterprise*, April 1958, p. 4: "Can we afford now to do business on any front, with the Soviets?"

103. *The China Story*, Chicago, Regnery, 1951; *Will the Middle East Go West?* Chicago, Regnery, 1957. See reviews in the *National Review*, December 28, 1957, and in the *New Leader*, January 6, with further comments January 27, 1958.

104. *The China Tangle*, Princeton University Press, 1953. Westerfield, *Foreign Policy and Party Politics, Pearl Harbor to Korea*, New Haven, Yale, 1955, esp. Ch. XII. See also Eric Goldman, *The Crucial Decade*, p. 116, quoting the late Senator Wherry: "With God's help we will lift Shanghai up and up, ever up, until it is just like Kansas City." There are, of course, many right wingers in the Democratic party, especially in the South, but these have usually, in the past, been less troubled about internationalism and foreign policy. It is true also that some Republicans from coastal states who are very conservative in other respects are willing to recognize Red China for the trade potential. See Westerfield, *op. cit.*, and *Exclusive*, September 17, 1958 about the danger of this to William Knowland's campaign for Governor of California.

105. An investigating committee of the U.S. Senate alleged that Owen Lattimore had worked as a "conscious articulate instrument of the Soviet conspiracy," according to *National Review*, March 29, 1958, p. 295. Cf. Westerfield, p. 251; p. 145. See also Ralph DeToledano, *Spies, Dupes and Diplomats*, New York, Duell Sloan, 1952; Owen Lattimore, *Ordeal by Slander*, Boston, Little Brown, 1950; John T. Flynn, *The Lattimore Story*, New York, Devin-Adair, 1953.

106. Hargis in *Christian Crusade Magazine*, March 15, 1958.

107. See the *Bulletin* of the National Renaissance Society, June-July, 1956, "What Adolph Hitler was to the Nordic Aryan people, Gamal Nasser is to the mighty horde of Islam. Many Germans who were loyal to the highest racial ideals of National Socialism can now be found in the ranks of Nasser's advisers and confidantes." See also *Closer Up*, November 30, 1956, and various issues from 1956-1958 of *Williams' Intelligence Summary*, *Common Sense*, *Women's Voice*, *The Defender Magazine*, *The American Nationalist*, the *Economic Council Letter*, *The Cross and the Flag*. Cf. the publications of the Arab Information Center, the Press Department of the Egyptian Embassy, the Organization of Arab Students in the U.S., the American Council for Judaism, the American Friends of the Middle East and the literature distributed by the Non-Partisan Voters' Committee for Eisenhower. Many of these groups distributed such pamphlets as *Murder, Rape and Devastation: Israel's Record in Sinai and Gaza*.

108. See Epstein and Forster, *Cross-Currents*, 1956, and Ralph Lord Roy's review

of this book. See also remarks of Norman Thomas, *New Leader, January 27, 1958*. It is difficult to understand why the American Jewish Committee and other official Jewish groups have never had the grace to acknowledge the very real contribution made to Jewish life in America by Elmer Berger and his American Council for Judaism; nor why Rabbi Berger, for that matter, could find nothing but good to say of Egypt on his recent visit there. The American Council, though listed as a conservative group by the *First National Directory,* is of course considered rather radical in other circles. See Berger, *Who Knows Better Must Say So,* ACJ, 1955.

109. See Fayez A. Sayegh, "Soviet-Israeli Relations," *American Mercury,* April 1958, pp. 69-80; James W. Fifield *Zionism vs. Judaism,* Los Angeles, Freedom Club, 1956; Alfred Lilienthal, *There Goes the Middle East,* New York, Devin-Adair, 1957, and *What Price Israel?* Chicago, Regnery, 1953.

110. *Economic Council Letter* No. 427, March 15, 1958. Hart mentions in this letter that those of February 10 and 13 have been reprinted in the *Congressional Record,* as well as in papers in Costa Rica, South Africa and Iraq, and that representatives of the Council have recently testified before Congressional Committees (p. 4). See Isaac Don Levine, "The Strange Case of Merwin K. Hart," *Plain Talk,* February 1950, p. 2: "The role played by Mr. Hart . . . may justly be described as that of a Trojan Horse. How else can one characterize a warrior, wearing the armor of Christianity, who is engaged in sowing confusion in the camp of those fighting for the ideal of human freedom for which Christianity stands? . . . He is in the business of merchandising anti-Semitism. And he wraps his contraband in packages bearing the labels of free enterprise, anti-communism and Christian love."

111. Philip Horton, "Rivivalism on the Far Right". *The Reporter,* July 20, 1961, p. 25-9; Alan F. Westin, The John Birch Society", *Commentary,* August, 1961, p. 93-105; Willie Morris, "Houston's Super Patriots", *Harpers,* October, 1961, p. 48-56; Gene Grove, *Inside the John Birch Society* "Fawcett Publications", 1961, 160 p.; there have also been several series of articles carried by many newspapers, as well as many other articles in *Life, Look, The New York Times Magazine* and elsewhere. Current developments have been adequately described in recent months.